Trench Warfare

ASPECTS OF WAR

Trench Warfare

STEPHEN BULL

PRC

Acknowledgements

Many people and institutions have helped make this book possible. First and foremost I should like to thank my father Barry Bull, who has supported this and all my other projects unstintingly, and with whom the subject of World War I has been a talking point for many years. The staffs of the Imperial War Museum; Lancaster City Museums; Lancashire Museums; and the Queen's Lancashire Regiment Museum have all been unfailingly helpful. Particular thanks are due to the trustees of the Queen's Lancashire Regiment for the use of a number of photographs and documents. Mr Andrew Brooks, Geoff Carefoot, and members of various branches of the Western Front Association and Great War Society have also made valuable contributions which deserve better thanks than can be expressed in these few lines.

Produced in 2003 by
PRC Publishing Limited,
The Chrysalis Building
Bramley Road, London W10 6SP

An imprint of **Chrysalis** Books Group plc

This edition published 2003
Distributed in the U.S. and Canada by:
Sterling Publishing Co., Inc.
387 Park Avenue South
New York, NY 10016

© 2003 PRC Publishing Limited

ISBN 1 85648 657-5

Printed and bound in Malaysia

CONTENTS

THE WAR TO END ALL WARS

Few wars have had as big an impact on the human psyche as World War I. Even those who were there and had most reason to loathe the war could be prisoners to its spell. It had what Guy Chapman of the Royal Fusiliers called a "vile attraction." Through much of Europe there are still monuments to the conflict. Not many are as poignant as the cemeteries of the Western Front: the shady German grounds with a few stark dark crosses and somber tablets, for so many thousands in a given acre; the French and American lawns with their serried ranks of brilliant white markers. Perhaps most moving are the British, tended by the Commonwealth War Graves Commission. These have individually crafted regimental headstones and consciously English-style gardens—usually on a human scale. Most shocking to the British eye is the ossuary at Verdun, where the curious may peep through portholes and see the actual bones of some of the unidentified French and German dead. It looks like disorganized archaeology, until you remember that this is also family history.

Every day hundreds, if not thousands of people ask archives, museums, and websites what their grandfathers and great grandfathers "did in the war." They unconsciously fulfil the prediction of Savile Lumley's famously emotive recruiting poster in which an embarrassed-looking character is being questioned by his daughter.

Only we now know that the vast majority did go, over five million of them in the case of Britain

Left: **Playing on a guilty British conscience.**

Below: **Still from the film** *Battle of the Somme*. **British troops go "over the top."**

Above: **The Flanders Offensive. Hauling an 18 pounder field gun out of the mud near Zillebeke, August 9, 1917.**

Right: **Troops of the 4th Australian Division wear small box respirators against gas attacks near Ypres, September 27, 1917.**

alone, and many never came back. It is also true that the little girl's question does eventually get answered. Unlike some earlier wars it is very often the case that the records of 1914–1918 are still there, and we are surprised to discover that the man in the photograph, with a face very much like our own, was "Mentioned In Dispatches," in some God forsaken pool of mud in Flanders. Despite another world war, with its much clearer objectives, this remains The Great War. "Battlefield tourism" of the sites of 1914–1918 is a now a well-established phenomena, and the war is a formally approved part of the British National Curriculum.

Odd artifacts of the trench war also surface to this day, and not only from the mud of Flanders, in the hands of metal detector owners with a death wish. Many families still treasure their ancestors' medals, others have a large brass medallion with a name and the figure of Britannia, sometimes not realizing that this was

struck to commemorate the dead. As recently as 2002, in the countryside near Tewkesbury, I was surprised to find a rum jar from the trenches that was standing completely unrecognized on a farmer's doorstep.

Surprisingly our interpretation of the war, and specifically of the trenches has changed as much with time as our thinking about the Greeks or Romans. One of the most influential early critics was Basil Liddle Hart, who had himself been an infantry officer. As he so waspishly put it:

"The Western Front idea of attacking the enemy at his strongest point and giving him every chance to develop his heaviest armament was not war, nor is it tennis."

A mere 20 years ago it was still accepted that the way World War I was fought was unremittingly and irredeemably stupid. Trench warfare battles were portrayed as consisting essentially of lines of troops emerging repeatedly from the trenches

Above: **Men of the Border Regiment resting in a front line trench, Thiepval Wood, August, 1916.**

into walls of machine gun fire. The winners were those with most men left—or American reinforcement. The best, and most thoughtful, of the then current literature, like John Ellis's *Eye Deep in Hell* (1976) and Denis Winter's *Death's Men* (1978), were essentially books about the diabolical conditions under which the troops had to labor. There were a few alternative voices, like that of John Terraine, but their counter arguments seemed based on limited evidence. Tony Ashworth, for example, argued that trench warfare was a "live and let live" system. It may have been in the quietest sectors, but this told us little about the mechanics of the conflict. This was also, considering the millions of dead, something of a self-limiting proposition.

Given this essentially negative background, the little buff manuals issued by the General Staff proved fascinating reading. The wonder was that these told a totally different story to the "approved" version of events. Far from accepting that trench warfare was monolithic and

unchangeable they were full of ideas: not all of them were practical, but they were demonstrable proof of a ferment of thought and activity aimed at finding new ways to survive, and even new ways to attack. The real shock was that these were not the musings of a maverick junior officer, nor the contents of a soldier's diary saying what he would have liked to have done, but official documents, even instructions. They were printed in thousands and widely issued. More intriguing yet was that among them were a good number of German documents translated into English. As primary evidence of what soldiers were taught to do, what they knew at the time, and what the army was trying to achieve, these were superior to any amount of self-justification contained in the memoirs of the famous. They also provided a template against which the individual soldiers' experiences could be measured.

The subjects covered in official publications included everything from infantry tactics, to signalling, trench foot, and "Strombos Horns."

At the time Guy Chapman of the Royal Fusiliers even claimed to have found one entitled, "Am I Being Offensive Enough?" Such a thing may never have actually existed—nevertheless the plausibility of its existence, and the fact that manuals on everything could become a joke, shows just how all-pervading such literature became.

For anyone studying contemporary official publications it is soon apparent that the conflict had seen the introduction of huge numbers of new weapons, and radically new tactics. Some things, like the Lewis gun and the Mills bomb, appeared to have made a contribution far beyond the mundane or periodic improvement that one might have expected in the normal course of events. They might perhaps have been a spur for a major shift. In 1986, in one of my earliest articles, the opinion was put forward that there had been "a revolution" in infantry tactics. An editor crossed out the word "revolution," replacing it with the more watered-down formula that finally got into print. A faltering attempt to make a

challenge to the then almost universal "stupid" view of the way the tactics of The Great War had met the immovable object of received orthodoxy.

If the "infantry tactics revolution" lobby has been proved wrong with the passage of the intervening years it is only because the case was vastly understated. There was a genuine revolution in infantry tactics, but this was just a small part of a far bigger upheaval in the making of war. The invention of the tank, the adaptation of aircraft to fighter and bomber roles, the advances in artillery, and the development of chemical weapons, were all as significant in their own way as the "minor" tactical changes that impinged upon every private soldier.

Though many of the original protagonists in the trenches, and notably Charles Carrington, Hesketh Pritchard, and Ernst Jünger did have an idea of the great transformations that were going on around them, the bigger picture has now been explored more fully by recent historians. Bruce Gudmundsson came to grips with the detail of

Below: **German stormtroops move up, supported by flame-throwers, near Sedan, May, 1917.**

Stormtroop Tactics as early as 1989. Yet foremost amongst the tactical studies of the last decade must be counted Paddy Griffiths' *Battle Tactics of the Western Front* of 1994, a book which has proved the most thought provoking on the subject for many years. Just a year later Martin Samuels' still controversial work *Command and Control* built on his earlier *Doctrine and Dogma*, which sought to contrast British with German methods.

What seems to have emerged in recent studies is a polarization between those who believe that the Germans were first and best with the "new tactics," and those who have it that the British were the original and superior. This makes for fascinating argument, but scarcely accords with the evidence. At the distinct risk of being in a minority of one, a strong case can be made for the fact that the relationship between the French, German, British, and finally American methods was essentially synergistic. A small detail would be improvised by one or other, then it would be copied, perhaps bettered, by the opposition. The copy might then be copied by the side that first "invented" the original idea. Nobody stayed in a dominant position for very long. Equally while Lewis guns were superior to German Maxims, particularly in the offense, the German snipers and flamethrowers stole early leads in other directions.

The British knew from experience the vital need for reliable grenades that were simple to produce, but the Germans got there first, only to be overtaken later. In the planning of defenses and use of concrete the Germans were ahead, but in tanks they were sadly lagging. German artillery seems to have been superior early on, but was overtaken—as was also the case with gas, and particularly gas defense. Had the war continued any longer, as it seemed that it might do, the Allied preponderance in tanks would have become even more obvious. On the other hand the German development of the submachine gun and

---

Below: **The 1st Lancashire Fusiliers being addressed by General de Lisle before the Battle of the Somme, 1916.**

Above: **German flame-throwers in action, 1917.**

the antitank rifle would also have gained a greater significance.

What may also be contended is that it was the rapid development of small unit tactics which had the most widespread, most significant, and most enduring impact of all the military changes during the war. The Private soldier entirely altered his behavior, became more self-reliant—and most importantly, had to make up his own mind to fight. No longer was the individual always within "voice control" of an officer or senior NCO. Usually he was with his peers, perhaps a Corporal, or a "Gefreiter"—and sometimes, as a scout or sniper, he might be alone. The lines of troops, at first almost shoulder to shoulder, were rapidly spread by gaps of yards. Ever thinner skirmish lines and "bombing parties" began to produce new sub-organizations. Individual officers within battalions assumed special

Left: **Sentry wearing a PH gas mask—the fabric had been impregnated with Phenate Hexamine.**

13

Above: **Snipers of the U.S.
168th Infantry in camou-
flaged suits at Badonviller,
May 18, 1918.**

Right: **German troops
throwing hand grenades
over a belt of barbed wire,
May, 1917.**

responsibilities for new areas. Snipers became a notoriously antisocial and workshy club of a dangerously unmilitary disposition. The "empty battlefield," already effectively cleared by the barrage, and the "beaten zones" of the machine guns, was finally repopulated by the new nuclear families of platoon and section.

The professional skill of the soldier was no longer limited to the endurance of the march and "point and shoot." Now there were myriad other possibilities: grenade throwing, entrenchment, and platoon action were well nigh universal accomplishments, but now a majority, rather than a minority, had to learn more. Rifle bombing, sniping, scouting, and the various machine guns were just some of the options, but "ordinary" soldiers could also be signallers, runners, gas specialists, tunnellers, and tank crew to name a few of the more obvious possibilities. More than ever before new officers were needed, and many rankers penetrated what had been a difficult barrier in peace time, crossing what was a substantial social divide. It may therefore be contended that it was the twin pillars of mass conscription, general on the continent but introduced in Britain for the first time in 1916, and the tactical and technological revolutions that made the biggest contributions to the democratization of war. The effects of this remain with us still.

To keep the war going, and morale high, the appeal had to be broad—to the patriotism, and to the consciences of the many. No longer would it be enough to persuade those who were financing the war, or had political interest, that the struggle had to go on. Those who were actually fighting it, their families and friends, had to be convinced, and for this the newspaper vendor and the bayonet instructor were equally in the front line. A majority, or at least a sufficiently influential minority, had to see the need to "keep right on to the end of the road." As Gary Sheffield put it, accurately if cynically:

> "...the greater the participation of a population in war, the greater must be the reward (or bribe) offered."

Neither British shopkeepers and mill workers, Aussie roustabouts nor American farm boys left their families to fight for anything trivial. This became the Great War for civilization, democracy, self determination, and "a land fit for heroes." In Britain the "Welsh Weasel," David Lloyd-George, first persuaded the public that this was so: then blamed the generals when they discovered that it was not. This perhaps is where the dive to disillusionment, with the war and war in general, really began. It is also, chronologically speaking, the point at which the seductive, but simplistic, idea of "Lions led by Donkeys" really took off.

Ultimately of course the peasantry, intelligentsia, workers, and finally the soldiers of Russia, Austria, and Germany, in that order, could no longer see the benefits of continuing the war. It was no accident that these were

Below: **Parliamentary Recruiting Committee poster from March, 1915.**

Above: **The 11th Hussars rest after the retreat from Mons, September, 1914. The photo shows Lt. Arkwright who was killed while flying, later in the war.**

Above: **Sniper of the London Irish Rifles, 1918.**

nations in which the democratic input into policy was either nil, or moderate.

It is also worth reflecting that it is the lot of the infantryman which has changed least since November 1918. Sniping, digging, grenade throwing, personal fitness, basic camouflage, and the skills of the junior leader are all pretty certain to have some place in November 2018. If we were able to pluck the victorious Tommy Atkins fresh from his triumph on the Hindenburg line, and drop him into a modern uniform, he would still have some inkling of what was going on. Great grandad would probably be accepted as a reliable, if quirky, member of the section within a month or two. The same could never be said of the scientists, fliers, or even the civilians. This then is a lasting practical military impact of the Great War.

Though common sense has largely prevailed in the revisionist versions of the trench war, we should not be tempted to become complacent.

There is a danger of a new orthodoxy—an accepted belief that World War I generals could do no wrong and that there were no genuinely pointless disasters. It should be equally obvious that there were many problems, and that some were actually insurmountable, given the social and technological world of that moment. There were horrendously bloody battles, errors of both commission and omission, and men died in unheard of numbers. The contradictory term "friendly fire" may not have existed in World War I, but the reality of being caught in your own barrage was all too well known.

As regards casualties they were made all the more shocking by their unprecedented scale. Rather more British soldiers died on the first day of the Somme, for example, than at Edgehill, Culloden, Waterloo, Balaklava, and Spion Kop put together. Moreover, the Somme went on, albeit at a less intense level than July 1, 1916, for over four months. Yet this is often the nature of

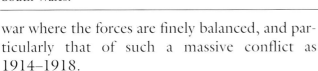

Above: **Australian recruiting poster from New South Wales.**

Above: **Australian troops disembarking at Anzac Cove in Gallipoli.**

war where the forces are finely balanced, and particularly that of such a massive conflict as 1914–1918.

With Gallipoli, the scene of some of the most difficult trench warfare, even the most doctrinaire revisionist has difficulty. A pet project of Winston Churchill, it is hard to see how this adventure could have made a very significant contribution to victory, even if all had gone well. If by the mechanism of some as yet unidentified miracle Constantinople had fallen, there is no guarantee that this would have caused Germany or Austria serious problems.

As we now know, post war Turkish collapse demanded British troops as peace-keepers attempting to fill a vacuum. Like as not similar occupation forces would have been required in 1915—to no productive purpose, as it is unlikely that the modest additional support available to Russia through the Black Sea could have ensured the Czar's survival. In 1915, when the war was going badly for the Allies on many of the existing

fronts, opening up a new theater with inadequate preparation or supply was at best a waste of time and resources.

To take another controversial example it is now frequently contended that those British soldiers shot for various reasons of military justice during the war were either totally innocent, according to the old school, or equally guilty according to the laws of the time and the revisionists. Neither view holds water, as may be seen from the detailed picture. Over 400 men were condemned for falling asleep at their posts, but only two were actually executed.

Courts Martial records, notably those of 1st Battalion the Royal Irish Rifles, suggest that this was actually just the tip of an iceberg. Many hundreds fell asleep at their posts, and it was very rare for a death sentence to be passed. A far more usual sentence was from two to ten years—sometimes commuted to various field punishments which served to keep the man in the line. At least one soldier aged under 18 was convicted of

Above: **Chinese laborers were employed by the Allies during the war; here at the port of Boulogne, 1917.**

desertion and later executed, but of course according to other rules he should not even have been on active service under age. Equal miscarriages of justice can and do occur, in peace time, in a civilian court. A good number of those "shot at dawn" were indeed innocent and hapless victims, in the wrong place at the wrong time. In some instances it was explicitly stated in the documents of the case that an execution which might otherwise have been commuted was carried out as "an example" to others.

On the other side of the coin more than a few of the soldier martyrs would have got themselves hanged had they stayed at home. Over ten percent of those soldiers executed, 36 other ranks and one officer, were put to death for murder. A sapper of the Royal Engineers, being ordered off parade to put on his puttees, quickly returned and shot his officer. Another man, having been absent without leave, came back to his unit and was put under close arrest. He shot his own platoon sergeant in the neck. Two workers from the Chinese Labour Corps robbed a French

estaminet, and in the course of their crime killed a French woman. They were executed just as they would have been in peace time London or Paris, and probably more humanely than had their offence been committed in China. In this, as in so many matters, there is no blanket answer, nor should we judge a world a century away by our own, often questionable, values. We have no right to expect simple, or generalized, soundbite solutions to complex historical questions.

Communications was an especially problematic area, fraught with potential disaster, which was never satisfactorily resolved. In fact the generals were faced with an impossible dilemma. They could remain at the end of a fixed phone line or near a transmitter, and get a very partial view of the war, at an headquarters where the food was excellent, and the casualties few. Or they could venture slowly to the front and see a couple of hundred yards of churned mud and attempt to encourage the few dozen men they would meet, some of whom might, or might not, appreciate the gesture. While there they would cease effective command, receiving any important message at the maximum speed a man wading through mire could achieve. There was no halfway house: no light and reliable radio system, no cable capable of transmitting visual images, no flitting in and out in a helicopter. It is little wonder that, having been killed in some numbers early in the war, generals tended to retreat to headquarters where they were of some, if intermittent, consequence to the proceedings.

Some of the worst catastrophes happened, neither because generals specifically ordered them, nor because there were no new tactics. Instances where wave after wave struggled into barbed wire, or were repeatedly machine gunned, or shelled by their own guns, were sometimes accounted for by a lack of intervention from on high. So many waves were timetabled, so many reinforces had to be planned in advance from point A to point B, that the least delay, or unforeseen event, could throw all into confusion. With

no quick communication the 1916 equivalent of a motorway pile up could go on for hours. The instances in which this might be accounted a genuinely criminal folly were where such hammerings were repeated week on week, or month after month, in full knowledge of the consequences and lack of result.

Such an accusation might be leveled at the continuation of the Somme battle. The grinding at Verdun was brought to a halt in mid-July and one of the major reasons for opening the battle of the Somme was thus achieved—whether or not one had directly caused the other. The tanks, which had been a good reason to reopen the attack on September 15, were not subsequently available in any great numbers during the latter part of the year. The objectives of late September, October, and early November are by no means clear, and the weather was bound to get worse. As the *British Official History* explained, not entirely convincingly:

Below: **Preparation for the the Battle of Arras, April, 1917. A Divisional Artillery officer observes fire and a Royal Engineers' telephonist passes back the results.**

Above: **The first American troops to arrive in England, 1917, made an impressive image but it would be mid-1918 before large numbers reached the front.**

"Although the Battle of Flers-Courcelette had not accomplished all that had been hoped, Sir Douglas Haig was convinced that the German reserves were now almost exhausted, and that the time was coming for General Gough to strike hard: indeed slow progress of General Rawlinson's right, dependent as it was upon the advance of the French, made vigorous action on the left of the British fighting front all the more desirable if the Allied pressure were to be maintained."

The failure of intelligence to properly access the enemy situation hangs unspoken in the air. Fortunately such things were not a general feature of the last year of the war, when more limited attacks in different sectors served to keep the enemy continually off balance.

The point about communication remains genuinely important today, if only because the modern democracies now seem to be going over-board in the opposite direction. A debate in a London suburb decides whether an Argentinean warship sinks on the other side of the world; a satellite mounted camera helps Washington decide whether an unmanned craft will act, or not act, over Iraq or Somalia. Every soldier seems likely soon to be wearing a headset which will tell him if the man opposite will live or die. The danger is the disenfranchisement of the man on the ground who is, or should be, responsible for his own actions and his interaction with those around him. Complex "rules of engagement" may cost him his life while saving votes. Technology appears to be making possible the ever upward passing of decision making. Perhaps the "Chateau general" is alive and well after all.

NATIONS AND SOLDIERS

World War I had many causes, and no simple solution. Germany, which would ultimately bear the blame for the war, was certainly at the heart of the matter. As recently as fifty years before the outbreak of the war there had been no state called "Germany." There were certainly "Germans" who spoke the language, had deep-rooted aspirations and historical traditions, but the nation was only formed, famously, by Chancellor Bismarck's "blood and iron" during the 1860s, culminating in the proclamation of William I as German Emperor in the Hall of Mirrors at Versailles in 1871. The new state had been forged in a series of wars, with Prussia pitted successively against Denmark, Austria, and France, emerging stronger after every round.

Even then the new Germany was theoretically a federal edifice, with no less than twenty-two rulers including four kings who had gathered together under a voluntary act of association. The very existence of Germany depended on Prussian military might and the Prussian king was emperor and head of the imperial executive, so Prussia was very much the preeminent force. Yet the new Germany was constitutionally complex. Its *Bundesrat*, or Federal Council, gave sanction to legislation, and though this was dominated by Prussia, the smaller members could have banded together to stop controversial law. The *Reichstag*, being a chamber elected by universal suffrage,

Below: German army pre-war maneuvers. The company in the foreground is drawn up in a thick line, with its officers to the fore.

was theoretically a highly democratic body, roughly equivalent to a parliament but its term of office was only three years. The Chancellor, responsible to the Emperor, was not actually obliged to act on *Reichstag* resolutions, and was therefore a highly significant figure.

Diplomacy, and the then accepted fact that war was the final arbiter of international dispute, had given birth to Germany. Until almost the end of the 19th century neither Germany's existence, nor its ambitions, had led to any crisis which diplomacy was unable to surmount. Moreover, through the *Dreikaiser Bund*, or three emperors' league, security was achieved on two of Germany's three main land borders. Yet the diplomatic blunders of later Wilhelmine Germany, made worse by Emperor Wilhelm II himself, would prove almost as spectacular as Bismarck's successes. Policy now went beyond local security, and hegemony over German speaking areas. This *Weltpolitik* threatened Britain in a

new way, but even this might not have put Britain into a position of direct rivalry had it not been accompanied by the start of a naval arms race. The successive German Navy Laws instigated by Grand Admiral von Tirpitz, and the launching of HMS *Dreadnought*, arguably the first modern battleship, in 1906, were just some of the most important landmarks of escalation.

With the deterioration of Russian–German relations new patterns of alliance began to emerge. While these were intended to increase individual security the linking system of obligations created a mechanism which encouraged the war, when it came, to spread rapidly. As early as 1892, a secret Franco–Russian convention, "animated by a desire to preserve peace" had set out the detailed circumstances under which each would come to the aid of the other:

1) If France is attacked by Germany, or by Italy supported by Germany, Russia shall employ all her available forces to attack Germany. If Russia is

Below: **German prewar maneuvers, the cloth bands on the helmets denote which "side" the infantry are on.**

Above: **HMS** *Dreadnought*, **whose launch in 1906 sparked an escalation of the naval build-up in Britain and Germany. Ironically, she never fired a shot in anger.**

attacked by Germany, or by Austria supported by Germany, France shall employ all her available forces to fight Germany.

2) In the event of the Triple Alliance or one of the powers comprising it should mobilize, France and Russia, at the first news of the event and without the necessity of previous concert, shall mobilize immediately and simultaneously the whole of their forces and shall move them as close as possible to their frontiers.

3) The available forces to be employed against Germany shall be, on the part of France, 1,300,000 men, on the part of Russia, 700,000 or 800,000 men.

In the event of war France could therefore hope not only to avoid repeating the humiliation of 1870, but by attacking vigorously in concert with friends regain the territories she had lost. If the somewhat paranoid nature of German diplomacy was one of the major causes of war, and the web of alliances served to raise the stakes, there was also plenty of other tinder around with which to build the conflagration.

Turkey's decline and the rise of national and Slavic aspirations in south-eastern Europe had already resulted in wars prior to 1914. Furthermore there was no ready indication that these complex internecine troubles could easily be resolved. In 1912, Greece, Bulgaria, Serbia, and Montenegro went to war with Turkey, soundly defeating her in the First Balkan War. The armistice reached after this opening round collapsed quickly, with a new bout of fighting between Turkey on the one hand and Bulgaria and Serbia on the other. The peace which followed the Treaty of London in May 1913 lasted only weeks before Bulgaria fell out with her

Above: **French infantrymen of the 161th Regiment. The full marching order worn included packs with cooking pots and the Lebel rifle. The black and white photo fails to reveal the soon-to-be-discontinued, red trousers.**

Above: **German reservist with G88 Mauser rifle.**

former allies, and Rumania took advantage by attacking Bulgaria in the rear. Turkey promptly began to seize back some of the lost territories. Britain was anxious that these relatively petty bush fires should not spread, but despite some temporary agreements both Russia and Austria had interests in the Balkans which would ultimately prove explosive.

That the war would become so big so quickly was not just the result of alliances. More than ever before, the Europe of 1914 was one of armed camps, and on the Continent conscription ensured vast standing armies. What would become the Allied powers had about three millions under arms. According to the *Handbook of the Russian Army*, Russia alone had 1.3 million men at the end of 1913. Her army had much recovered since the debacles of war with Japan a decade before, though poor infrastructures were likely to be a handicap. France had enacted ever

more draconian laws designed to keep up a big army despite a static population. The "Three Years Law" of 1913 set out a scale against which the conscript did three years with the colors, followed by no less than 25 years as a territorial or reservist who could be recalled from his normal occupation in time of war. The result was a standing force of over 700,000 with plenty of scope for increase. Her infantry were primarily schooled in the art of attack, and her 75mm field guns were numerous and famous for their extremely rapid fire—a short burst of up to 20 rounds in a minute being claimed by some sources. Belgium had a surprisingly large army for such a small nation, and Britain, though initially dependent on her relatively small professional force at the outset, still deployed about 90,000 as its first commitment.

Germany had a standing army of about 840,000 at the outbreak of war, and efficient

Above Left: **British soldier of the Durham Light Infantry wearing regulation Service Dress and Pattern 1914 leather equipment. The short magazine Lee Enfield rifle is fitted with the 1907 Pattern bayonet with its 17 inch blade.**

Above: **Russian troops in greatcoats and fur caps. Unlike most other nations, full Russian decorations were worn with the field uniform.**

Left: **Austro-Hungarians, including a bugler.**

mobilization enabled the immediate deployment of reservists in the front line fighting force. The Kaiser, though notoriously vacillating and prone to veer wildly between peace and war, had pushed two significant technological advances in the German army. The first of these was Krupp-manufactured guns of the latest types. He had backed General Staff Quartermaster Alfred von Waldersee in pushing for a build-up of the artillery, and has been famously cited as dismissing no less than three ministers of war for their obstruction. The second was an uncharacteristically clear and far-sighted embrace of the machine gun. Exceptionally Wilhelm was actually ahead of his generals in this instance. During a visit of Prince Edward in 1894 a demonstration was held at Spandau. Maxim's gun fired over 300 rounds without hesitation: prompting the Kaiser to pose melodramatically with his finger on the piece and state, "That is the gun—there is no other." Though previous German tests had led nowhere,

Wilhelm insisted that the question be reopened. Mystified officials passed a few machine guns on to the artillery, who had little use for them, then to the Jäger battalions. After 1904 and the Russo-Japanese war it was belatedly appreciated that the "all highest" had been correct.

On the debit side the Kaiser's personal influence also had a number of distinctly negative impacts. In several turn of the century army maneuvers Wilhelm had insisted on leading one of the opposing forces, and umpires had been understandably reluctant to find their sovereign was on the losing side, even when he used totally unsuitable tactics. In 1903, for example, he had ordered the entire cavalry corps to make a mass attack from a distance of roughly three miles. He was declared the winner of this particular war game despite the fact that a prepared infantry brigade and massed artillery stood in his path. Though Wilhelm had remarked on the lack of uniformity in infantry tactics he had signally

Below: **German machine gunners with a model 1901 Maxim gun. By the outbreak of war there were two per German battalion, mainly of the 1908 type.**

Above: **Austrian Archduke Franz Ferdinand and his wife, Sophie, Duchess of Hohenberg, are about to get into their car, where they will be assasinated by Serb Gavrilo Princip, Sarajevo, June 28, 1914.**

failed to intervene decisively to sort this out, and had erred on the side of encouraging mass close order attacks when such had already proved disastrous on the battlefield.

The well-known spark which actually ignited the conflagration of the summer of 1914 was the assassination of the Austrian Archduke Ferdinand at Sarajevo. Yet the spark was very nearly a damp squib. Austria issued dire ultimatums and Russia and Germany fumed, but war was almost averted when Serbia attempted to mollify Austria's demands. France, in any form of sane arrangement, should have had very little to do with the crisis as she had no common border with any of the key protagonists. Britain took active steps to attempt to prevent the outbreak of war—and even the Kaiser showed significant qualms when the moment of decision came. Yet planning,

alliances, and even common public expectations tipped Europe over the edge. What had originally started as the Third Balkan War soon became World War I.

The pictures of cheering crowds, greeting and waving off exuberant soldiery, are accepted as defining images of the war of 1914. Yet as with so many aspects of the period, this is also an over simplification. Research by Jean-Jaques Becker on original data collected by French teachers at the time suggests an altogether more complex reaction. The need to mobilize for example, was more frequently described as a "grave" or "sad" development, than as a happy event. Only when actual mobilization took place, and the troops were departing, did the French rise to the occasion with a show of enthusiasm and high spirits. Even then there are many who were

Right: **The 2nd Battalion Royal Warwickshire Regiment is transported by London buses through Dickebusch to Ypres, November 6, 1914.**

Below: **Recruits waiting in the rain to join up at the Whitehall Recruiting Office, 1914.**

putting a brave face on resignation, and eye witnesses recorded women in tears. Interestingly the questions of Alsace and revenge were mentioned only by a minority of ordinary people in such accounts.

Nevertheless many volunteered who did not need to go, and this was probably most apparent in Britain where there was no compunction. With the exception of Dublin the major cities were bringing in men by the thousand. London alone would soon have 42 recruiting stations, and so busy were they that doctors and clerical staff worked them in shifts. A single hour at the main Great Scotland Yard office alone produced as many as 100 volunteers. All told, about a third of a million men were enlisted in the first month. The recruiting base covered many different classes, as Lieutenant Colonel Cobb of the 5th Battalion Oxford and Buckinghamshire Light Infantry recalled of his unit:

> "There were a great many from respectable homes and businesses. Some gentlemen, many indoor servants, grooms, gardeners, chauffeurs, gamekeepers, well to-do tradesmen, hotel-keepers etc., etc., to say nothing of the engineers, fitters and hands from the great works in Birmingham and Coventry. All these men had left good comfortable homes, with good wages, and had come voluntarily out of a sheer sense of duty."

Statistical work by Peter Simkins confirms this impressionistic snapshot: one in five in many occupational groups had enlisted within eighteen months. Among educated professions the numbers were even higher: bizarrely entertainers were the best represented group of all with a remarkable 41.8 percent of the entire male work force joining up.

In his recent book *Forgotten Victory*, Gary Sheffield has claimed that though a staggering 22 percent of the male population of the United Kingdom served in the army, this "did not represent a true cross section of society," and that "some geographic areas produced far more recruits than others." The single example used to support this contention is a battalion of the Devonshire Regiment, a specific detail already noted in Peter Simkins *Kitchener's Army*. Beyond

the obvious point that areas with small populations could not possibly produce large numbers of men, this is a profound misunderstanding of the regimental system—which meant, and still means so much to the British Army.

The connections of infantry regiments with counties were predominantly established in the 18th and early 19th centuries, and the depots of those of the county regiments which existed in 1914 were fixed during the reforms of the 1880s. Since the Industrial Revolution saw the bulk of the population move from the country to the towns between 1700 and 1900, it was inevitable that there would be little agreement between population density and regiments. Even this is but part of the story, since we know that the correlation between the title of the county regiment and the origin of its men was often sketchy. Men could, and did, enlist for units other than those of their native area. There are even well-documented instances where soldiers deliberately left their home area, so

Above: **Lucky escape: a British woman holds a soldier's paybook and the bullet that penetrated it. Many wives would have a less satisfactory outcome.**

as to be less easy to find, or to fabricate their age without fear of discovery.

To take but the most famous example, we are aware through the meticulous work of Norman Holme that the defenders of Rorkes Drift in 1879 had little to do with Warwickshire, and not much more to do with Wales, even though they were from the 24th (2nd Warwickshire) Regiment, later the South Wales Borderers. Of the majority of men whose origins we know 27 came from all parts of Wales; 42 from parts of England other than Warwickshire; and 13 from Ireland. Just four are definitely known to have had connections with Warwickshire, including the great city of Birmingham. The idea that Rorkes Drift was won by cockneys and scousers does not settle easily, but it does make an important point that the Edwardian drill sergeant would have understood.

Before the war there were no ready made communities of suitable men ready to become the backbone of the army. The regiment took all manner of types, often misfits, and by means fair or foul, welded them into the "regimental family." Some of the methods were what we might now call "hard" management—bullying, various punishments, and raucous shouting on the parade ground. Others were softer, and probably more successful, like regimental traditions, sport, ale, martial music, and the comradeship of shared experience. It was the Territorials, and even more particularly the "Pals" battalions of Kitchener's "New Armies," who were genuinely different to this long-established picture. Some, at least, were already in recognizable groups. Hence the battalions of stockbrokers, artists, public school boys, post office, tram workers and sportsmen—even the so-called "Grimsby Chums."

Another significant point is that, particularly later in the war, geographical mixing was actively encouraged to prevent the burden of loss falling too heavily on any one area. Similarly wounded men did not always go back from whence they had come. The case of 1st Battalion Royal Irish

Below: **Kaiser Wilhelm, foreground left, and his six sons—all in uniform. The Crown Prince (1882–1951), wearing the hussar busby, is next to his father.**

Der Kaiser mit seinen 6 Söhnen.

Phot. B. I. G. Berlin

Rifles, as elaborated by James Taylor, makes an interesting, if particular, example. With Irish recruits drying up, Englishmen, especially those from London, were used to top up the ranks to the point that only about half of the men were born in Ireland. When all recruits were in short supply the rear area troops were "combed out" and many men from the Army Service Corps found themselves in this notionally Irish regiment. The official War Office publication *Soldier's Died in the Great War* gives us perhaps the best snapshot of the origins of a large sample of men. Very often the regular battalions had a significant number of men from the home county; but equally a large mixture from elsewhere. The most homogeneous were the largely volunteer contingents who made up the battalions of the "New Armies."

New drafts certainly did not, as a matter of course, flow smoothly from the regimental recruiting area to the matching battalions in the field. The 11th Battalion of the Loyal North Lancashires, sent replacements to its own regiment, but also to the Rifle Brigade and Machine Gun Corps. The 12th Battalion of the East Lancashire Regiment sent troops to various other formations including the King's Liverpools, and even sent men to a munitions factory. Norman Collins, who volunteered for the Seaforths in 1915, recalled that his particular hut had only three men "with Scotch relations" while of the 30 men next door there was only one. For some obscure reason the Yorkshire "twang" was the commonest accent.

There is good reason to suppose that, particularly after conscription, the main groups that did not see service were vitally necessary munition and agricultural workers, the disabled, the very unfit, the very young, and the old. Even in these categories there were those who succeeded in reaching the front. The sixteen year old who pulled up to his full height and answered "Nineteen Sir!" when asked his age is a well worn cliché, but many such people certainly existed in fact. Robert Burns of the Cameron Highlanders was just one of many. Failing to

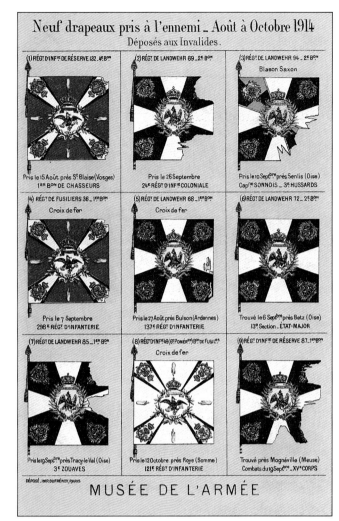

Above: **Nine enemy flags captured by the French in the first three months of the war, subsequently deposited at the Army Museum, Paris.**

enlist at the first attempt he went home and mysteriously gained a year in two weeks. The manager of his new company told him it would be "a nice six month holiday." George Maher, who worked at Horrocks Mill in Preston, failed to impress at his home town recruiting station, but by taking the train to Lancaster managed to join the King's Own. Lieutenant Cloete, with 9th Battalion the King's Own Yorkshire Light Infantry, claimed that his best sniper turned out to be only 14 years old when his parents finally tracked him down to get him discharged from the army. He was "big for his age," and went by a false name, but had shot six Germans by the time authority caught up with him.

Less well known are the genuinely "old soldiers" who slipped through the net. Most amazing are those select few born before the Crimean War. Claimed as the oldest authenticated example is Lieutenant Henry Webber, who was serving as transport officer to 7th Battalion the South Lancashire Regiment when killed on the Somme in 1916. He was 68, and thus older than most generals and indeed Germany itself. Herbert McBride, an American serving with the Canadians, noted that his own unit varied in age from 16 to 52, and that there was "probably considerable lying" at either end of the scale. Some of the older ones had medals for campaigns in India which were over long before some of the youngsters were born.

What the disabled could achieve is also remarkable. Quite how many managed to make doctors turn blind eyes may never be known, but a few cases have come to light for various reasons. Several infantry regiments boasted distinguished one-armed or one-eyed officers. Lieutenant Colonel Merriman of the Royal Irish Rifles, twice wounded in the Boer War, lost an arm in 1915. This disability in no way precluded several mentions in despatches, and later command of a battalion. Another 20th Hussars officer was wounded, and only then was it discovered that previous injury had left him with one leg much shorter than the other. Thereafter he was kept at home: until he succeeded in joining the Royal Flying Corps where his walking difficulty was not seen as a drawback.

As might be imagined, clothing, arming, and even housing the great human tide of early volunteer recruits was beyond even the resources of the first industrial nation. The result was a sprouting of temporary hutted towns, the use of church halls, and tented camps. The prospective troops, like Joseph's coat, were in a positive rainbow of colors. Some stayed in their civilian suits; many wore blue; a few gray, and some wore obsolete full red dress. Even when supposedly official khaki first appeared there were variations, as in

Below: **A British postcard, delivered in 1914, points out that many Irishmen joined the British army. The humor would be less apparent by 1916 when the Easter rebellion severely stretched resources.**

Begorra, but ye thocht Oi was going to be a thraitor.

Above: **German soldiers clear up the carnage in a wood on the Eastern Front. It is not always remembered that the Russians suffered 1.7 million dead on a front which remained more fluid than the West.**

the case of locally manufactured uniforms for Welsh troops which seemed to vary from distinctly green to chocolate brown. Henry Ogle, who volunteered and was accepted for 7th Battalion of the Royal Warwickshire Regiment was fortunate to get the proper khaki uniform quickly, but viewed it with some disdain:

> "The color was a filthy browny yellow designed with complete success to look like mud or dust. It buttoned right up to the neck, where the wide, down-turned collar gave no relief or transition from square body shape to round head shape, almost hiding the neck so our faces stood out on our collars like badly done puddings. The ugly flat service cap was simply 'putting the lid on them.'"

In the early days of the war there was no such thing as being fitted for uniform. Tunic, trousers, and puttees were literally thrown to the recruit after he had been "sized up" in the time it took to walk from the door to the table. However there was no regulation against swapping, and bad misfits got sorted out sooner or later. Active service proved the uniform not as bad as it looked.

The British personal equipment was of three main varieties—completely obsolete sets from the Boer War which were fortunately changed while still in the UK; the leather 1914 Pattern produced as a war time emergency measure, and given mainly to "New Army" units; and the standard 1908 Pattern webbing kit. Again Ogle struck lucky with the 1908 webbing, but when he was handed the thirteen assorted straps and bags:

> "It was realized with a slight shock that these bits and pieces had to carry everything that the soldier possessed except the rifle itself and the clothing one stood up in. That is to say: bayonet and scabbard, entrenching tool and handle, water bottle, 150 rounds of .303 ammunition in thirty clips, mess tin, hold-all with its personal cleaning gear, cutlery, iron rations, jack knife, cap-comforter, towel, rubber ground sheet (6 x 3 feet) and lastly (and voluminously) the greatcoat."

Recruits were shown how to assemble the parts of the equipment and, to their enormous relief, how to reduce the greatcoat to a neat rectangular bundle which could be stevedored into the pack.

33

Above: The "Kitchener Blue" uniform worn by men of "C" Battery, Royal Field Artillery, 103 Brigade, 23rd Division, during the erecting of tents at Mytchet Camp, Aldershot, 1914.

Though the total 61lb load, including clothes and weapons, was undeniably heavy, Ogle was pleased to find that the equipment was well designed and "carried it well." The main pack was often discarded, and the small pack worn on the back reducing the load considerably. Moreover, "It was incomparably better than the wretched leather gear."

THE STRATEGY

The trenches which would eventually lock solid the entire borders of France and Flanders from Switzerland to the sea, and the admittedly more fluid lines of the Austro-Italian frontier and Eastern Front, were by no means the deliberate strategy of any power.

Indeed, there was a well-nigh universal assumption that it was offensive action which held the key to victory. Alfred von Schlieffen had thought that any war had to be short since a long war would be impossibly expensive. The Kaiser's famous statement to his troops, "You will be home before the leaves have fallen" was widely remembered—and also widely believed. The expression "Over by Christmas," summed up the expectation of a quick war, and many men were anxious to join up quickly, precisely because they imagined the fighting might be over before they had managed to reach the front.

Against this general premise there were few dissenting voices but there were some highly significant warnings from Lord Kitchener who thought a three year was possible, and from Moltke who said that a war would be a "people's war," potentially "long and wearisome." Other German Generals who had at various times suspected that a war might be much longer than the common assumption included General Staff Quartermaster Friedrich Köpke, and Baron Colmar von der Goltz head of the Corps of Engineers. Goltz had repeatedly approached the Kaiser years before 1914 with plans that would have been useful in a long war scenario. These included ambitious fortress construction, which

Below: **Italian troops emplaced in the mountains of the Alpine front against Austria. Though the Western Front is most associated with trench warfare, entrenched positions existed in virtually every theater.**

was doubtless dismissed as personal empire building on his part.

In the event financial systems would prove more robust than anyone had imagined: the war could be protracted on credit. While monetary considerations were put aside in Germany, Britain effectively mortgaged the war. Income tax, itself a relatively new phenomenon, paid only about 20 percent of the running costs while the war continued. Similarly the human material of war proved supple and durable in the face of horror. High casualties led to local setbacks and surrenders, but not to any swift breaking of national resistance. Industries and economies were progressively harnessed to the struggle, and even those countries least adapted would last a surprisingly long time.

Turkey and Russia, with some outside assistance, would be good for three years, Austria for more than four. Germany, even without control of the seas, lasted still longer, as did France, despite mutinies in 1917. Britain, which had husbanded her human resources in 1914, eventually planned 1919 in some detail, and had some thoughts on continuing during 1920. A black joke which circulated among British troops had a punchline referring to grandchildren coming up to the front during the 1960s.

The basis of German strategy was the now infamous "Schlieffen Plan"—the essentials of which had been drawn up by Field Marshal Graf Alfred von Schlieffen, Chief of the Prussian General Staff, as early as 1905. Hitherto it had been supposed that if Germany should find herself at war with both France and Russia, she would stand on the defensive in the west while attacking Russia. Schlieffen held many paper exercises and wargames trying out various possibilities. These included attacking eastward; waiting on the defensive in the west followed by counterattack, and enveloping entrapments around French forces which attacked in the center. None of these seemed to answer the basic problems. Any long war appeared doomed to

Below: **The defenders of Germany's borders: the pride of infantry regiment 138.**

failure. So, as a piece in the *German Military Weekly* put it:

> "Our only salvation is to strike down the nearest and most dangerous enemy before others can intervene in the fighting."

Thus it was that Schlieffen had put forward a radical new strategic departure, as bold or bolder, than the glories of 1866, 1870, or Blücher's forced march to Waterloo in 1815. Under the new scheme the vast bulk of Germany's might would be thrown against France, with the overwhelming majority of the force falling on the northern part of the line. By massing the strength in one area Germany would achieve vital local superiority, and make rapid headway. By keeping

Left: **Female munitions worker—or "munitionette"—from a Gloucestershire factory. The demand for shells and stores of all descriptions brought about a remarkable, if temporary, revolution bringing many women into new work places.**

Below: **View of the howitzer shop in the Coventry Ordnance Works.**

Above: **The Kaiser's call for sacrifice.**

Above: **General Pavel Rennenkampf, commander of Russian First Army, 1914. Early progress into East Prussia and the fight at Gumbinnen worried the enemy command, but his defeat at the Masurian lakes eased German fears.**

the right wing strong, with three-quarters or more of the mobile force available, a huge right hook could take the invaders right around Paris, leading to an early end to the war. Actual capture of Paris might not even be necessary, since by striking a part of the enemy with the bulk of the German army such a catastrophic defeat might be occasioned near the border that the French might sue for peace.

Part of the reasoning was that Russian mobilization was likely to be slow. The Russian rail network was ill placed to bring the Russian steamroller over the border quickly, while Russia itself was a vast arena in which to gather armies or conduct campaigns. Under such circumstances it seemed possible that comparatively light German defensive forces in the east could delay the Russians enough to make a disproportionate contribution to the final victory. This daring but essentially simple scheme was an elegant solution, which appeared to have

mathematical beauty in the face of difficult odds.

Yet the plan entailed several problems which were not obvious at first sight. One consideration was that the numbers of men in European armies increased between 1905 and 1914, just as technology continued to advance in ways which made a bold sweeping attack less plausible. machine guns increased in numbers and distribution, and larger numbers of the latest artillery pieces were deployed. Observation aircraft made large scale movement more likely to be detected. Even after retirement Schlieffen himself realized that weapons were becoming progressively more effective, and that this might have a bearing on strategy as well as tactics. Writing in 1909 in an article entitled "War in the Present" in *Deutsche Revue*, he came to the somewhat complacent conclusion that though technology had advanced, most armies had essentially the same weapons. Therefore the advantages and disadvantages balanced. With hindsight we can see that they did not: advances in projectile weapons and numbers of men in trenches were not squared by equal improvements in mobility and battlefield communication. Though it may not have been immediately obvious, defense was going to have the upper hand.

Importantly the Schlieffen Plan also made certain the very fear that it was designed to dispel: for in any war sparked in the east, France would now be immediately enmeshed. The Kaiser belatedly inquired whether the move west could be halted while an aggressive posture was advanced in the east. It could not. As far as Britain was concerned many Germans, including Schleiffen, could not quite bring themselves to believe that a fight would be provoked over Belgium. In the instance of British involvement the only obvious answer seemed to be to make the right flank ever stronger and ever faster. So it was that he demanded at least 45 divisions to enter Belgium and swing around onto the French flank. The question of possible British involvement was especially frightening because it made a short war even more imperative. Perhaps Britain might not engage with land forces, but though the German Imperial Navy was much expanded there was no guarantee that foreign trade routes could be kept open. If the Royal Navy was in opposition, it was calculated that Germany had but nine months before shortages would begin to bite hard.

The traditional shortcoming put forward for the Schlieffen Plan is that the way it was actually carried out was but a dilution of the original concept. As revised by Moltke the right wing was proportionately weaker than had been envisaged. Moreover since the Belgians fought tenaciously and took time to overcome, detailed redeployments became necessary. Eight divisions had to be diverted to deal with Antwerp and other places, while worry about the situation in the east led to the siphoning off of a further four divisions from von Bülow's Second Army. Casualties at Liege, Mons, and elsewhere have been computed as accounting for the equivalent

Below: **Russian medical personnel. Four men in each company were trained as stretcher bearers, and every four-battalion regiment had its own, small medical staff of surgeons, "dressers," and orderlies.**

of three divisions. So it was that the "sharp end," hooking into France on the right, equated to about 22 divisions at the vital moment of decision—a margin of superiority too slender to allow a decisive victory.

The French Plan XVII, issued in February 1914, was aggressive in the extreme: but in the event would fare even worse than the more famous German scheme. The essence of Plan XVII was that:

"Whatever the circumstances, it is the Commander in Chief's intention to advance with all forces united to attack the German Armies. The action of the French Armies will be developed in two main operations: one, on the right, in the country between

the wooded district of the Vosges and the Moselle below Toul; the other on the left, north of a line Verdun-Metz."

Having smashed the main German force in this frontier battle, and secured Alsace, the way would now be clear for an attack deep into German territory. It was not subtle thinking. As Basil Liddle Hart once famously observed, Plan XVII was the sort of effort that "the humblest *poilu* would have provided in return for a pint of *vin ordinaire*." In addition to wholehearted endorsement of offensive action there were two features of the French strategy which demand further comment.

One is that the plan was not really new: as early as 1911 Foch had put forward a study

Below: **The German invasion plan gambled on a quick end to the war. A long war on two fronts was the nightmare scenario.**

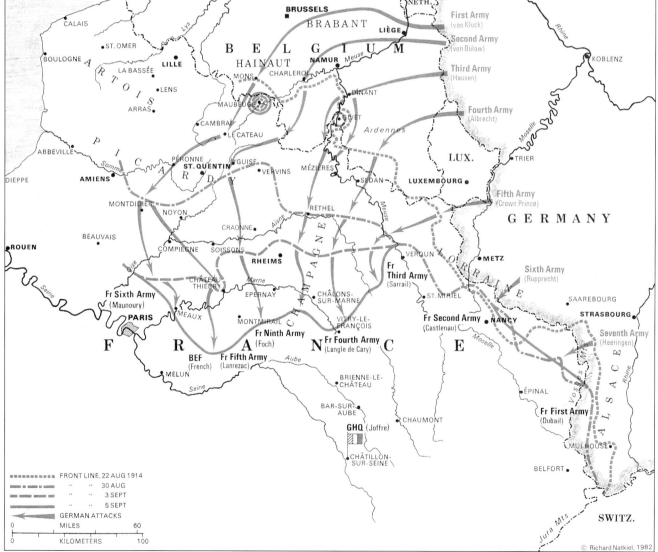

Above: **Belgian infantry ready for the first clash of arms.**

Left: **The occupation of Brussels; German horse-drawn transport passing through the Boulevard Baudauin, August 26, 1914.**

Right: **The Battle of the Lys: French cavalrymen pass through Hesdin during the German offensive, April 14, 1918.**

Below: **Tsar Nicholas II blesses his troops, 1915.**

recommending a general advance between Belfort and the Ardennes. In this he had pointed out that, what was to his way of thinking, an overly-defensive mentality in 1870 had led to disaster. Fortresses, as he put it, had a way of becoming "tombs of the Armies." Most importantly, "there is only one way of defending ourselves, that is to attack—to attack as soon as we are ready." Only retrospectively, in post war memoirs, would he question the "one magnificent formula" of attack. The other significant factor was that the Belgian frontier featured but little in French thinking. Indeed, when terms such as "right" and "left" appeared in strategic plans these were applied essentially to the northern and southern portions of the Franco-German border. Nevertheless it was appreciated that the enemy might attempt some envelopment of the left flank. Against the eventuality of a violation of Belgian neutrality, the French Fifth Army was to maintain a reserve. It could move north east, or turn to protect the flank, but such maneuvers would be carried out, "only by order of the Commander in Chief."

Russia was the wild card in the equation. It was assumed she would be slow to mobilize. The German gamble was that events in the west would be decided before significant intervention could be made from the east. Lack of rail lines, long distances, weak administration, and creaky resupply systems were parts of the problem.

Conservatism in the Russian army, extreme even by the standards of the time, was similarly an issue. Cavalry was a numerically larger part than in most armies; fortress guns absorbed a significant slice of the artillery budget, and the relationship between infantry and artillery was ambiguous. In the opinion of General Danilov the Russian people were also "psychologically unprepared" for war.

> "The *moujhik* went to war because he was accustomed to complying with an order given him by the authorities. Passive and patient, he was used to bearing his cross till the time of great trials."

Even so, Russia's population of 170 million was a massive potential strength. Her recovery from war with Japan and the internal disturbances of 1906 was complete. Ordinary defense expenditure rose steadily each year from 473 million roubles in 1910 to 581 million in 1914, and additional capital sums were spent on specific projects. In terms of pure numbers Russia had more guns than Germany. A "Great Programme" for 1914 postulated further army expansions, and sent ripples of worry through Berlin. By the outbreak of war Russia not only had a bigger army but was spending more on its support.

It has also been noted that Russian mobilization did not necessarily mean war, since it was possible for her to maintain her force within its own borders for some time. The idea of a selective and partial mobilization which would threaten Austria–Hungary, but not Germany, was even put forward. Yet this would have been almost impossible to achieve since it was a deliberate policy to include a mixture of the different races of the Empire within various formations. To prepare one frontier for action would have entailed mobilizing a patchwork of oddments over vast areas. Though theoretically desirable such subtlety was clearly impractical. Similarly it would not have pleased Russia's French allies, who had recently provided grants for the improvement of Russian military infrastructure.

Though less well known than the French and German plans, the Russian strategy, revised in 1910 as Plan 19, and further modified in 1912, was critical to the way the war would unfold. Contrary to previous models which would have held back much of the army in a defensive posture, it was now assumed that offensive action would take place as soon as possible. The major areas of activity were to be East Prussia and Galicia, designed to take account of Germany and Austria-Hungary respectively. Though with hindsight this division of strength was self defeating, early intervention on German soil would have significant repercussions. Merely by invading, the Russian contribution was to divert German resources from the critical point of decision at a vital moment.

It has been said of Joffre that "by sacrificing Plan XVII. . . scuttled the Schlieffen Plan." This has more than an element of truth. As his General Order of August 25, somewhat coyly admitted,

Right: (*From left to right*)
General Joffre, President
Poincare, King George V,
General Foch, and Sir
Douglas Haig meet at
the Chateau Val Vion,
Beauquesne, August
12, 1916.

Below Right: **Battle of
Pilckem Ridge: 11th
Durham Light Infantry
being taken forward
by light railway, July
31, 1917.**

Bottom: **Troops detraining
at Poperinghe, September
30, 1917.**

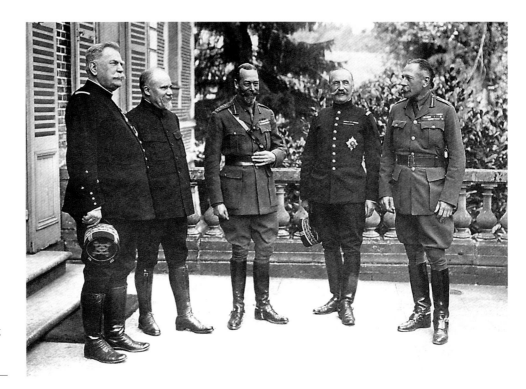

the "offensive maneuver" previously planned had
"not materialized." As a result subsequent operations were to be aimed at building up the left
wing, as a preparation to future offensive action.
By accident or design the French armies stopped
pushing at the "revolving door," and jammed a
foot in front of the bulk of the Germans on the
Marne who were now beginning to wheel in
front of Paris in an attempt to cut off the French
forces from the capital. Though the "Miracle of
the Marne" may have been overstated, the first
days of September marked a significant water-
shed. With the armies of D'Esperey, Foch, de
Cary, and the British holding the front
Manoury's Sixth Army was now poised to turn a
flank. After days of heavy fighting Moltke took
the momentous decision to disengage and the
Germans retired across the Marne. Moltke himself was quietly retired from his post and replaced
with von Falkenhayn on September 14, a change
to be publicly confirmed later.

Though grand, strategic considerations were
undoubtedly important, there were also technical
and material factors acting against a swift decision
in 1914. The power of the latest weapons to
sweep troops from the landscape, and the huge
numbers involved were also highly significant.
Traditionally there had been plenty of room for

maneuver in Western Europe—armies of tens, or at most hundreds of thousands, had been able to march around one another, while communications systems often failed to warn of attacks in time. Railways now allowed troops to move faster than ever before—and even transfer from front to front with a fair turn of speed—yet this rapidity was not one which transferred to the battlefield itself. Soldiers arrived at the nearest railhead which had not been destroyed and were promptly reduced to walking speed. Actual battles and potential breakthroughs were still conducted at a Napoleonic tempo, while troops moving longer distances to intercept these offensives could move much faster. The result was that strategy tended to disappear all too easily into a form of tactical treacle. Sweeping moves up to a frontier were very possible if properly planned and timed—moves beyond degenerated into a foot slog every bit as exhausting as those of previous centuries.

A major paradox of the attack was that denser formations generated more firepower, but at the same time presented an easier target to hit. Moreover if the men spread out it became more difficult for officers to control them. Though several nations, notably the British, had experimented with what the Germans called "Boer tactics," in many of the early actions troops were committed almost shoulder to shoulder. These were what Foch, with hindsight, would call the "blind and brutal" tactics which were so often "unproductive of results and costly." As early as 1915 A.H. Atteridge would note that:

"The Germans argued that a denser firing line would crush out the fire of its dispersed opponent and inflict loss not only on the men in action, but on the supports reinforcing them. We have seen the result of this theory of the fire fight in the battles of the present war, where the Germans have invariably pushed forward closely arrayed firing lines, which gave our men the impression they were 'coming on in crowds.'"

Lieutenant Hodgson of the Royal Artillery was

Below: **German troops advancing on the Western Front.**

Above: **German troops on the march in 1914. The rapid advances of the early months of the war showed the determination of the German infantryman.**

on the receiving end of just such mass attacks at Le Cateau:

> "The German infantry appeared almost in front of us. There were hordes of them! They were in very close formation and they were coming forward... The order was shouted, 'Gun Fire!' That meant that all the guns had to fire at a speed of six rounds a minute. You can imagine the casualties they took. Men were falling down like ninepins, but still they came on. But their tactics were that they moved forward a few paces, dropped to the ground, then fired and then came on again. They were close enough to shoot at us with rifles, and we were firing back at point blank range. Of course this created sheer pandemonium."

Though there were indeed huge losses, it cannot be said that there was a lack of appreciation of the tactical problem. In 1914, French soldier Marc Bloch recalled that while his regiment moved in columns on the roads, as soon as they were within range of the enemy the formation was changed, "to one of platoons" four lines abreast which "the regulations prescribe for troops approaching the line of fire under threat of enemy artillery." As early as August 24 that year Joffre had circulated an instruction that in taking any strong point French infantry should be held back under cover during preliminary bombardment, and when attacking should only rush from a distance at which they would be sure to reach their objective. They should, as he put it, be "organizing themselves with a view to survival in battle."

It is also true that even in prewar exercises the German tacticians had not usually seen battles simply as a headlong shoulder to shoulder rush. Rather, charges would be used when they were thought to have a chance of success: otherwise an attack might be a series of hops up and rushes forward, and dropping down to shoot when needed. The man against projectile problem had also engendered lively debate. This was largely between those who said that the only possibility was a quick, manful push into the hail of bullets, which would put a swift end to the enemy, and those who said that a more circumspect approach was more likely to succeed. The latter school stressed rapid digging in, and working round the enemy flanks.

It is sometimes forgotten that the early battles of "open warfare" were particularly bloody—bloodier even than much of the trench warfare that followed. Frenchman Marc Bloch recalled that immediately after the battle of the Marne his comrades looked grave, but content:

> "Content with what? Well, first content to be alive. It was not without a secret pleasure that I contemplated a large gash in my canteen, the three holes in my coat made by bullets that had not injured me, and my painful arm, which, on inspection, was still intact. On days after great carnage, except for particularly painful personal grief, life appears sweet."

The sense of relief, the happiness of still being alive, was repeated many times on both sides of the line. Yet this deliverance was often tempered with disillusionment, and a realization that this was not going to be a war like any other. As German philosophy student turned soldier Alfred Buchalski wrote home that October:

> "With what joy, with what enthusiasm I went into the war, which seemed to me a splendid opportunity for working off all the natural craving of youth for excitement and experience! In what bitter disappointment I now sit here, with horror in my heart! . . . I should like to give you a complete picture of the whole battle, but only isolated incidents thrust themselves into the foreground. It was ghastly! Not

the actual shedding of blood, nor that it was shed in vain, nor the fact that in the darkness our own comrades were firing at us—no, but the whole way in which a battle is fought is so revolting. To want to fight and not even be able to defend oneself! The attack, which I had thought was going to be so magnificent, meant nothing but being forced forward from one bit of cover to another in the face of a hail of bullets, and not to see who was firing them!"

We sometimes think of the "Battles of the Frontiers"—of Mons and the Marne, as being somehow cleaner and more decent, more romantic even, than the trench war that followed. Any such conception is at best illusory—any sort of war having much the same sorts of life and death decisions. Corporal Lismore, a decorated member of 1st battalion the East Lancashire Regiment, faced a dilemma at Le Cateau which must have been replicated many times during the war, but can seldom have been reported in print:

> "This NCO was possessed of an iron nerve given to few, as before leaving the sunken road a badly wounded man, conscious but in awful agony,

Below: **French Dragoons armed with Berthier carbines and heavy cavalry swords c. 1914. Ornate helmets and swords would prove worthless in position warfare.**

Above: **An Austrian machine gun post high above the snowline in the Alps.**

begged him to shoot him. Corporal Lismore, after obtaining permission from his officer, put his rifle to the man's head and fired."

Later in the war Seaforth's Lieutenant Norman Collins claimed he was actually taught how to administer the coup de grace with a revolver, while kneeling behind the wounded man, talking to reassure him. He never did it—but wished that he had had the courage to help a friend in pain.

Failure of both the Schlieffen Plan and Plan XVII left both sides in a strategic vacuum. Falkenhayn viewed the German position with down to earth realism. Heavy casualties were compounded by an inability to reinforce quickly from the railheads which were now five days

march in the rear. Surprise was lost, consumption of munitions "exceeded peace time estimates many times over:" a continuation of the major offensive to end the war promptly was clearly out of the question.

Even so it was not possible to leave the German right, or northern, flank hanging in the air. To do so would have invited the enemy to walk around it. So began a series of northward maneuvers with the idea of "firmly establishing the right flank on the sea." This would later become known as the "race to the sea"—but in view of the damage and dislocations the armies had suffered it was more of a crawl, by means of a series of jabs. With this complete, a Western Front would be established from Switzerland to the sea.

THE TRENCHES

That the Great War—so long anticipated—would so quickly degenerate into a troglodyte struggle for holes in the ground was neither expected, nor welcomed. In all armies "normality" was movement and maneuver, not static defenses. As the *British Official History* remarked:

> "... none of the belligerents entered the war prepared for trench warfare on a large scale. Digging had been encouraged by precept in the British Army, but, owing to the rapidity of the course of peace maneuvers, was seldom possible in practice."

Nevertheless it was accepted that use of the spade or entrenching tool was a significant part of the soldier's duty, though historically it was the least glamorous. For many such work was not "proper soldiering" and came as a surprise.

Yet with strategic movement at an end, at least in the west, the power of modern weapons was making the surface of the battlefield untenable for men of flesh and blood. Even localized redeployments were becoming less and less viable under artillery fire as was reported in the very first edition of the British official *Notes From the Front*, 1914:

> "It has been found that the long range of the enemy's artillery combined at times with the

---

Below: **Textbook German *Schutzengraben*, or fire trenches, with traverses to limit the effect of shelling. Note the diggers in their off-white fatigue uniform.**

Bei den Armierungs-Soldaten! Der fertige Schützengraben

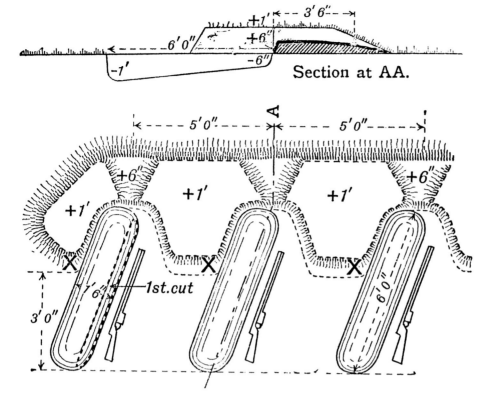

Section at AA.

weakness or even the absence of our own cavalry has rendered the infantry of the advanced guards particularly liable to come under artillery fire in close formation. Not only do the troops themselves suffer on these occasions, but the first line transport has been found particularly vulnerable … it is, therefore, essential… that troops should be able rapidly to adopt formations suitable when under artillery fire."

The same was even more true of troops actually attacking the enemy:

"An advance should not be made in rigid lines, but with clouds of skirmishers—five or six yards apart—thrown forward according to the ground and available cover."

According to one report from a British artillery officer who was attached to General Headquarters, the German artillery could only be described as "uncanny" necessitating many changes of position. Furthermore:

"… seventy percent of our casualties are said to be due to artillery fire, and most of them to the high explosive shell. The 'error of the gun' appears to be

virtually non-existent, and it is quite common to see four high explosive heavy shells dropped within two or three yards of each other…The enemy's time fuses are also astonishingly accurate."

Machine guns were proving similarly vicious, as *Notes From the Front* put it, the enemy was "very adept in making use of their surprise effect, which has been found to be very great indeed."

The necessity of digging in was accepted well before 1914 was out, to quote from *Notes From the Front*:

"Owing to the accuracy of the enemy's artillery fire, it is desirable that ground which is to be held defensively or to assist further advance should be entrenched. Trenches should be commenced at once with the light entrenching tool and improved later as opportunity occurs. They should be deep and narrow and should show above ground level as little as possible, and all trenches should be traversed at intervals of five to ten rifles."

Though each man carried his own entrenching tool, battalion picks and shovels were carried in a wagon and often left behind when the troops advanced, making it more difficult for them to dig in on arrival. It was therefore suggested that

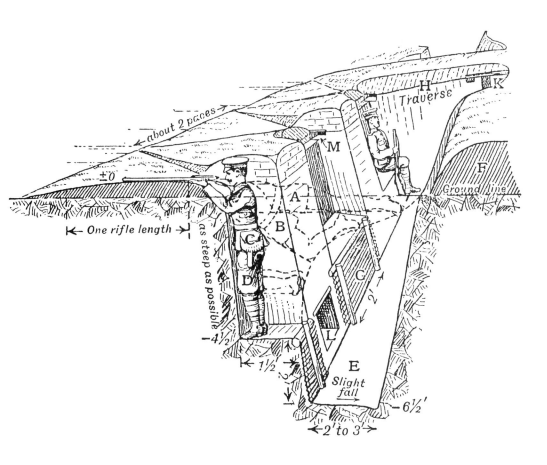

Left: The fully-developed field work with bays and traverses, as illustrated in E. J.Solano, 1914.

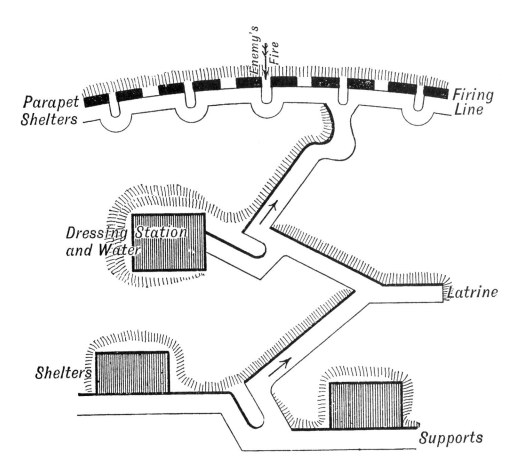

Left: Plan view of one of the first basic trench systems, showing a fire trench with shelters under the parapet; dressing station, latrines, shelters and support lines to the rear, as illustrated by E. J.Solano, 1914.

Above: **Maintained with concrete sandbags as a lasting memorial, the German front line trenches on Vimy Ridge.**

"at least 200" picks and shovels should be distributed among the men before they went forward. In emergencies, tools were requisitioned from local farms. So it was, as one Private of the Artist's Rifles put it, that the infantryman became "a soldier by day and a navvy by night."

The locating of trenches was sometimes haphazard, being where an advance ended or a retreat was finally stemmed. Nevertheless the most useful were placed with far more deliberation. The three major considerations were the protection given, the degree to which the trenches themselves could be concealed, and the field of fire. British regulations in force at the outbreak of war were insistent that defenders' weapons should be used to their maximum, and that attackers should be subject to fire for at least the last three to four hundred yards during their approach. Sadly trenches with commanding positions also tended to be those which were most easily spotted. As time went on greater emphasis was therefore placed on concealment, and fields of fire as short as one to two hundred yards were

declared perfectly acceptable. Some of the best defensive positions were proved to be on reverse slopes, completely unobserved by the enemy. Scattered and well-concealed posts on the forward slope would provide sniping opportunities and give warning of enemy intentions. Fields of fire could be further improved by the felling of trees or burning of crops. A subtle addition, noted specifically by Fritz Kreisler, was markers in front of the defensive position which would give the precise range of the attackers to the defenders. These could be bundles of hay, "or other innocent looking objects" which would not give the game away until it was too late.

So it was that the first lines of trenches appeared: surprisingly slender works compared with what would follow. As the *British Official History* noted:

"Before the frosts—the sides of the trenches stood vertical and without revetment; in fact they stood so well that it was even possible to obtain additional cover by undercutting the sides in the South African

Left: **On the opposite side of the same line, the Canadian trenches at Vimy. Note the loophole plate set in the furthest sandbag wall.**

Below: **The Scots Guards dig in, using shovels, near Zandvoorde.**

fashion, thus forming the first "funk holes." The trenches dug at this period were rarely continuous, usually a succession of pits capable of taking a few men. Generally they were of the narrow type, eighteen inches to two feet wide, with tiny traverses, three to six feet wide. These days were afterward spoken of in jest as the "Augustan Period" (August 1914) of field fortification. The narrow trenches, though giving good cover, were easily knocked in by high explosive shell, and proved the graves of some of the defenders, for men were occasionally buried alive in them."

Before the end of 1914 one staff officer recommended that the essentials for the infantry to learn were now, in order of importance: entrenching, rapid fire, covering their trenches from view of enemy artillery, bringing enfilade fire on enemy trenches, and skilful use of machine guns. A variation on the entrenchment theme was to use trench digging as a way to creep attackers forward to an advantageous position before going "over the top"—just in the way sappers of old had crept up to the walls of fortifications. Such methods were used in the run up to Loos in the autumn of 1915, and it is recorded how men of the 47th London Division spread out at night "like mice" from the sap heads, taking the utmost care not to jangle picks and shovels together as they got into position. Then,

as Lieutenant Waterlow of 19th (County of London) Battalion remembered:

"The men with the picks got to work at once, while the men with shovels lay at full length on the ground, with the shovel blade in front of them to protect their heads until their turn came. Never have I seen men dig at such a rate! They seemed to be two feet deep in no time. The policy was for each pair of men to dig a hole to give them as much shelter as possible and, when this was the required depth, to join up the various holes into one continuous line of bays and traverses. By a marvelous piece of good fortune we only had desultory rifle fire from the Boche."

The letters of Captain Billie Nevill, written in 1915, give examples of just how extemporized some of the early trenches could be, yet still exhibit the odd home comfort:

"Our parapet is very odd in places as it is revetted, or supported, with bedsteads, sideboards, table legs, cartwheels, bricks, fenders, and any old thing you can think of. Our dugouts are too killing for words. In one of them is a lovely case of stuffed birds, a beautiful four-poster bed, and some nice chairs, a good big table, towel horse, ivory wash-hand stand etc."

Gunner Paton recalled a somewhat slipshod Royal Artillery dugout in which the back wall

Right: **Australians in a trench shelter.** As *Notes for Infantry Officers on Trench Warfare* observed frames for such dugouts were often prefabricated behind the lines.

Examples of the Use of Portable Armoured O.Ps. in Trenches for Sentries.

Armoured Sandbag O.P.

Concealment and protection for British observers in the trenches, from a manual printed in the latter part of the war.

Hood of Painted Transparent Canvas used for Scouts or looking over Parapets.

Armoured Turf O.P.

Right: **Gas sentry ringing an alarm bell near Fleurbaix, June 1915.**

Below: **German soldiers reading by candle light inside a bunker. Such an existence made possible the holding of the line during bombardment.**

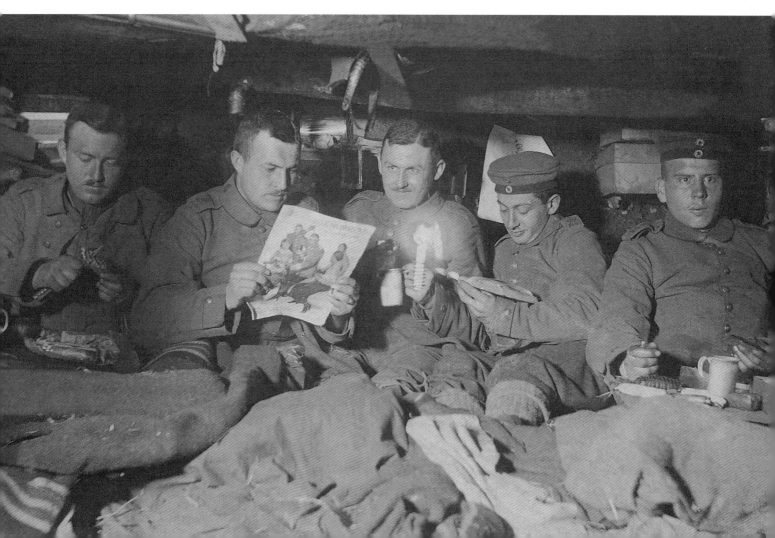

appeared to be revetted by means of a gray sand-bag. Here an officer would sit back in his chair at idle moments and rest his head. This was of course a great joke to the men who constructed the post, since only they knew that this was no sand bag but part of the uniform of a long dead German who was still inside.

Front line shelter from falling missiles was at best rudimentary in early excavations. Small "funk holes" tunneled into the trench wall closest to the enemy were the most common cover. The Germans gave these rat holes a far more noble name—the "Siegfried" dugout, but the effect was similar. In some sectors, particularly on the Eastern Front, where the war never became completely immobile, the trench systems would remain very basic—new lines being dug whenever the need arose.

The early French trenches have a particular reputation for being but cursory excavations, and if the recollections of Sergeant Marc Bloch are correct this may have often been deserved. Relieving the 128th regiment in La Harazée valley under shell fire:

"We were disappointed to discover only sharp-shooters' foxholes, disconnected from one another, too narrow to hold more than two men, and so shallow that to be sheltered one would have to lie practically prone. Our predecessors could hardly have blistered their hands on the handles of their shovels."

On another occasion Bloch occupied a trench which became "a brook" in the rain. When the rain stopped the men tried to light fires in the hope of drying their drenched clothes.

Intriguingly entrenchments and bunkers exhibited subtle variations in style according to precise location and nationality. Lieutenant Edmund Blunden, serving with 11th Battalion, Royal Sussex, made a tour of French works in the same spirit as one enjoying architecture or archaeology while on holiday:

"Large logs by the roadside speak of former French activity here; our own engineers do not make their dugout with such timber. The mildew-ridden bomb store also has a French style, and is full of

antiquated cricket ball grenades and others with tennis bat handles which we had best leave alone. Outside, on a kind of gallows, hangs a church bell, beautifully dark green, the gift of some fantastic ancient 'seigneur de Mailly' as its fair engraved inscription boasts. Perhaps the giver would not be wholly indignant if he knew that his bell was being used (as another inscription in chalk advises) as a gas alarm; for doubtless he intended it for the good of humanity."

Sometimes soldiers succeeded in making themselves surprisingly comfortable. German soldier Franz Blumenfeld wrote home as early as December 1914, to describe his dugout in which a stove for cooking and candle lighting had been contrived. The result was "astonishingly snug and pleasant."

Not long after came the extraordinary interlude of Christmas 1914. The Pope had had already appealed for a truce during the season of peace and goodwill—and Germany at least had accepted this premise. Though the idea was not formally accepted by the Allies many soldiers were determined to have a good Christmas, and at this time many Tommies bore "brother Bosche" very little real malice. The worst of the U-Boat war and Zeppelin bombing was still in the future—and poison gas had not yet been used.

The singing in the opposite trenches led to applause, and this led to tentative signals or shouts, and to suggestions for a pause to bury dead. On the sector of the 6th Battalion, the Gordon Highlanders, a joint burial service was held. Elsewhere British tobacco and chocolate was exchanged for cigars and German brandy. In at least one place there was the bizarre spectacle of Fritz and Tommy engaged in football. As Ernie Williams of the Cheshire Regiment remembered:

"The ball appeared from somewhere, I don't know where, but it came from their side—it wasn't from our side that the ball came. They made up some goals and one fellow went in goal and then it was just a general kick about. I should think there were about a couple of hundred taking part. I had a go

Above: **Northumberland Hussars meet their German counterparts in no man's land in the famous Christmas truce of 1914.**

at the ball. I was pretty good then at nineteen. Everybody seemed to be enjoying themselves. There was no sort of ill will between us."

Heavy frozen ground and ungainly army boots did not prevent what one NCO of the Cheshires called a "rare old jollification." At the end of the day quite a few men on both sides showed a distinct reluctance to go back to trying to kill one another. Handshaking as soldiers returned to their own holes in the ground was by no means unknown. In some places men attempted to organize "return matches" for New Year's Day, or exchanged promises not to shoot until a certain time on Boxing Day. The commander of C company of 1st Battalion of the North Staffordshires informed his Saxon opposite number that he had orders to start firing at midday on December 26: with both sides duly warned to keep their heads down at the appointed time, a few shots were fired, and quiet reigned for the rest of the day.

In one or two instances the impromptu peace even lasted until December 27 or 28. Some relatively senior officers winked at the temporary cessation of hostilities on the grounds that it was actually a good opportunity to strengthen defences, or gain intelligence about the troops that faced them and enemy trenches. Such attitudes went down very badly at staff level, and so frequently the war was kick-started again with a combination of shell fire and aggressive orders from above.

Though trenches were often well-planned, the effects of shells could turn even the best into chaos. Cameraman Lieutenant Geoffrey Malins took a close look at bombarded positions at Neuve Chapelle in 1915:

"We went along to the old German trenches, and during the whole time we bent nearly double, to keep under the line of the old parapets. In the old German trenches the frightful effect of modern shell fire was only too apparent. The whole line, as far as one could see, was absolutely smashed to atoms. Only the bases of the parapets were left, and in the bottom of the trenches was an accumulation of water and filth. It was a disgusting sight. The whole place was littered with old German equipment, and while wading and splashing along through the water I saw such things, and such stenches assailed my nostrils, as I shall not easily forget. Dotted all over the place, half in and half out of the mud and water, were dead bodies."

Deep cover was at a premium for resistance to shells. Cellars and dugouts reached by steps were ideal: some of the German positions on the Somme were reached by flights of 30 or more steps down. Yet in many instances improvisation took over where text book planning left off. At Zillebeke men of 118th Siege Battery, Royal Garrison Artillery, discovered a burial vault underneath the ruins of the church. Only some of the individual coffin recesses were occupied, so the gunners crawled in. As Gunner Paton recalled

the "quick and the dead" slept side by side for three months. Some of the best deep cover positions were seen by Private E.N. Gladden of the Northumberland Fusiliers, near Hill 60, in 1917. Here both sides had already realized that conditions were "hellish" and reduced their front line garrisons "to a string of strong posts," holding only the support lines in force:

"There was, under the hill on the British side, a wonderful system of saps and dugouts, a veritable underground settlement. The concreted and sandbagged posts above ground were joined by wooden stairways to the narrow bunk-lined sleeping quarters of the forward troops. Further down, passages lined with wooden planks led to larger barracks, and here were the headquarters offices and dressing station, so far below the level of the ground that the heaviest shell bursting above caused but a distant tremor through the galleries. The whole place was illuminated by electric light and the chug-chug of the pumps keeping water out of the galleries

Below: **German trenches in a wood near Langemarck, after the British bombardment, June 11, 1917.**

continued day and night. The company had come down from the front line into deep support as it was called. We occupied one of these billets, a cavern divided into two stories by a shelf some four feet from the ground and large enough to house a whole platoon. We slept, when we had the chance, in two layers…"

One potential disadvantage of deep cover from shells was that if the enemy succeeded in entering the trench while the garrison were still below ground, they could be bombed out, or forced to surrender. This is apparently how Private Thomas "Todger" Jones of the Cheshire Regiment managed to capture a mass of German troops in a celebrated incident at Morval in 1916. As one of his comrades observed:

"As he went over, a bullet went through his helmet and three through his coat, but he took no notice.

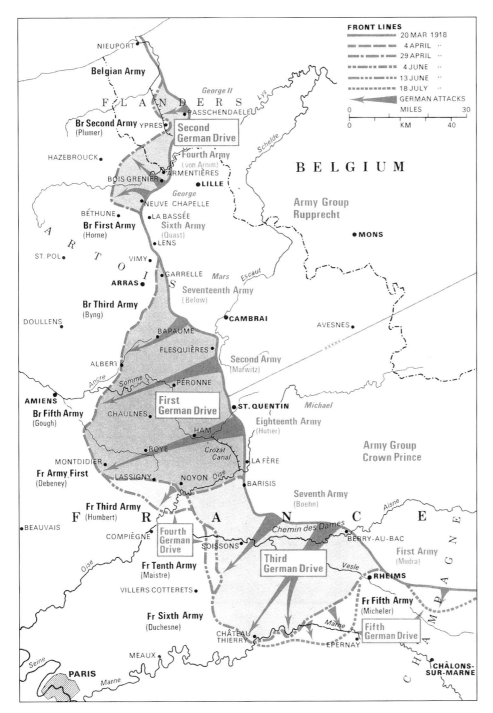

Left: **Map showing successive German advances through the spring and summer of 1918.**

Far Left: **Kept as a tourist attraction and memorial after World War I: a section of trench at Hill 60.**

Above: **Germans using earth-boring machines.**

When he got into the trench he got three of them straight away, and started to settle them as he met them. They bolted into their dugout and commenced to pop at him from the doorway... He flung a bomb down the nearest dug out and three came running out with their hands up... He told one of the Germans to tell his mates to come out of the dugout one at a time and any man who came out with arms would be shot. They came out, and when his chums came across they said it was the finest sight they had ever seen."

A total of well over a hundred Germans eventually emerged to surrender. Even though some fell victim to shelling while under escort to the British lines, 102 Germans were taken into captivity. Todger Jones became one of only two Cheshires to win the Victoria Cross.

From the opposite perspective German officer Ernst Jünger would see that the comfort and security afforded by very deep dugouts, where even some of the heaviest shells "made no more than a pleasant rumble," was sometimes bought at a high price. Those at the deepest levels could have as far to climb as the stairs of a four storey house to reach the surface. Thus it often happened that they had a warm reception halfway up from bombs and burning phosphorus without being able to strike a blow, particularly when the men on guard in the trench had long since given their lives in its defence without anyone below being any the wiser.

By 1917, the use of really deep bunkers near the front line trenches was being discouraged. One practical alternative was the use of shallower dugouts, proofed against shells by means of different materials. Concrete, corrugated iron, wood, and soil used in strata could be used to form a "bursting course" to detonate projectiles, and shock and fragment absorbing layers. By such means, good protection could be given against shells up to about the six inch caliber, with the troops only a few feet below ground and thus able to reach the surface quickly.

The idea may have long predated 1914, but World War I would see more widespread use of

Above: **The Arras Offensive: 9.2 inch howitzers in action near Arras, April 1, 1917.**

camouflage than any conflict to date. Khaki and gray uniforms were already widely worn, and even the French, hitherto wedded to their blue uniform and distinctive red trousers, changed to a less obvious "horizon" blue in 1915. This however was but part of the story, since with the realization that anything that could be seen could be destroyed, gradual efforts were made to camouflage virtually everyone and everything. As early as September 1914, Guirand de Scevola, a French artist serving with the artillery had hit on the concept of using painted canvas screens for the concealment of guns. By February of 1915 a French experimental detachment was employed specifically on camouflage projects, one of the first of which was to disguise an observation post as a tree. Thereafter, a camouflage service was formed with Scevola at its head and imaginative projects included dummy dead horses and men which hid observation posts.

The British army followed suit later the same year, starting with a small group of scenic artists, carpenters, and other specialists. This would be expanded into the Royal Engineers "Special Works Park" in March 1916. In addition to painting artillery pieces, the unit was soon working on a wide range of projects designed to make parts of the manmade trenchscape disappear. These included observation posts under various guises, acres of painted canvas, wire netting, and "fish net" camouflage screens, canvas robes, and dummy figures. Unusual efforts included the making of dummy canvas tanks, and eventually even concealment for aircraft hangers. Quantity production was achieved by mechanizing the processes and setting up dedicated workshops in France using female labor. Some idea of the scale of this effort can be determined by the fact that the British alone used over 4,195,994 square yards of scrim, and 7,493,856 square yards of "fish net."

Practical advice on what to do, and more importantly not to do, in the trenches was passed from battalion to battalion. Advice passed from men in the Durham Light Infantry to the Royal Warwickshires at Houplines, in 1915 and was remembered by Henry Ogle as follows:

> "Don't gaze over the parapet but use the loopholes and, if you are not a sentry, you have no business to gaze about anyway. Don't loiter anywhere and, if you are off duty, get into your shelter. Don't volunteer like a stage hero for jobs you know nothing about. If you do you may wreck the job. On the positive side there is a lot to learn—how to improvise cooking and washing, to make the best of rations provided, to use, make, and maintain proper latrines decently, to keep trenches and shelters clean and dry, to keep oneself and one's mind occupied usefully and intelligently, and if you really have nothing to do, get down and sleep."

Despite frequent inspections, keeping clean was almost as impossible as keeping dry or warm. If one succeeded in keeping vaguely warm then lice became a constant torment. Some thought they were worse than Jerry since, "you shoots 'im or 'e shoots you," but the "little bastards" were ever present, causing itching and scratching. As Henry Ogle recalled:

> "In billets there could be no peaceful sleep without the nightly 'chat.' 'Chatting' consisted of hunting the beastly things, first in the clothing, then on the person, and killing them without mercy between opposed thumbnails… One practice was to singe all round the underclothing seams with a candle flame. Some men even cut off all hems."

Ernest Parker of the Durhams was certainly not unique when he gave up the struggle with his lively underwear and threw it away. Edmund Blunden remembered dugouts near Beaumont Hamel with "probably the lousiest blankets in all Christendom." His own cover had the satisfaction of depth, but depth and warmth had a price since scratchiness came with the menagerie that shared his abode. The men referred to this place as "Ocean Villas," though pedants who studied the official maps saw "Auchonvillers."

Below: **Royal Garrison Artillery gunner washing at the entrance of his dug-out, Montauban, September, 1916.**

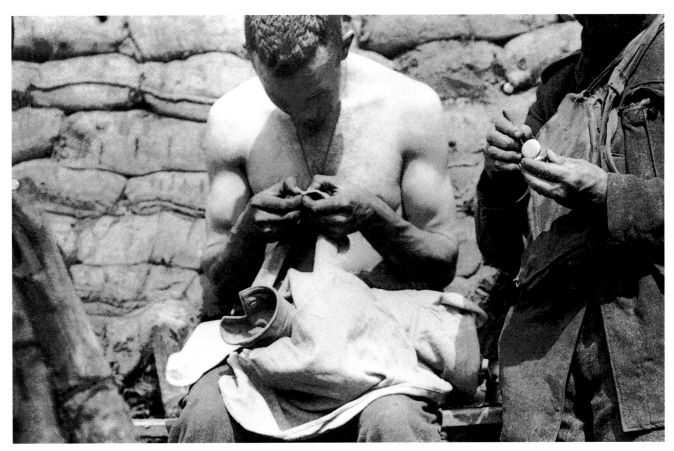

Above: **Looking for—and eliminating—the scourge of the infantryman stuck in the trenches: lice.**

A soldier with a rival claim to Blunden's blanket was a Gunner of 118th Siege Battery nicknamed "Lyddite." According to his comrades he was forever wriggling inside his clothes, and there was serious worry that the garments would creep away of their own accord. In any case he was so infested that no others would share his dugout, and the officers would order him to be bathed and his hair shorn forcibly. Nevertheless he drew the line at washing his underwear, with the result that he was given a relatively mild form of field punishment which included carrying provisions up to the front line. It was thought that he had been a tramp in civilian life and was merely carrying on a similar lifestyle in the army.

Robert Burns of the Cameron Highlanders recalled that the Royal Army Medical Corps laid on baths of a sort when barrels were available, filling them with water and a stringent disinfectant which turned the water white. Such efforts might kill the lice temporarily, but if clothes were not cleaned at the same time the infestation would return very quickly. Memoirs of the Machine Gun Corps refer to the highly organized efforts of the baths at Nieppe, where soldier and clothes were separated. The jacket and trousers were tied together with the man's identity disc and deloused. Meanwhile the soldier spent five minutes in hot water, followed by a quick hosing with cold, and the issue of fresh underwear and shirt. Man and clothing were then reunited, but if anyone was unable to find his deloused trousers, he "wandered round like a lost sheep" until provided "a pair yards too big, which he had to wear until he could arrange to rip them beyond repair on the next wiring party."

Flies could also reach plague proportions, covering dead men and animals in summer. Yet on the Western Front they were mainly a nuisance: in Gallipoli they were often potentially fatal disease carriers. As Dick Barron of the RAMC recorded:

"During the day when the rations came up, the flies swarmed. They were almost cloud-like and anything sweet or edible, they used to descend on it ... You could hardly get a mouthful of bully beef to your mouth before it was covered in flies. You waved your hand over them or lit a cigarette and blew the smoke onto the food to chase the flies away... where they went to at night I don't know, but within an hour of sunrise they came back again and caused as many casualties through disease as the enemy action, particularly dysentery."

Whatever their nationality or previous social station, life for troops in the trenches had a primitive quality which was almost universal. Violinist and Austrian soldier Fritz Kreisler described how all luxury, culture, and "refinement" disappeared—and amazingly how little he missed them. "Centuries drop from one, and one becomes a primeval man, nearing the cave dweller in an incredibly short space of time." He recorded a period of 21 days without taking off his clothes, sleeping in rain or mud, with nothing but his cape to cover him. Contrary to popular

opinion not all headquarters were immune to the squalor. Lieutenant Colonel N. Fraser-Tytler of the Royal Artillery was forced to take refuge a couple of miles behind the lines at Montauban in late 1916. He found the artillery headquarters in:

"... a sorry plight; their mess, office, and all dugouts were collapsing with the incessant rain, and there was already about two feet of liquid mud on all the floors. The camp beds were just clear of the water, and, as the Colonel remarked, 'if one had seen a tramp in the old days spending a night in such quarters the wonder would be how any human being could stand it,' yet we've all had nearly a month of such a life, and have become absolutely accustomed to it. Orders are typed out, beautiful maps made with etching pens and colored inks, all the old routine is gone through, even though everything and everybody are sticky with glue-like clay."

One dictionary definition of "trench foot" is "a diseased condition of the feet owing to

Below: **Trench foot was not a problem for the Australian troops entrenched around Anzac—seen here using periscopes. However flies and the frequent bouts of dysentry they helped spread, was just as disabling.**

exposure to cold and wet"—but this hardly does justice to either its variety or its potential seriousness. Some cases were a complication of frostbite: in others wet was the major culprit. *The Lancet* suggested that "water bite" might have been a more accurate expression—but the makeshift term trench foot stuck. It now appears that in either case cold was a key factor—with the body reacting by shutting off circulation in the extremities worst effected. In many instances a period out of the line was sufficient to cure a problem before it became too advanced, in others, toes had to be amputated.

In British statistics for 1915 there were six instances where trench foot was recorded as a cause of death out of the 6,462 trench foot cases, in addition to 16,256 cases of more general frostbite. As a medical officer, double VC winner Noel Chavasse took a professional interest in the problem as it first appeared among the men of the Liverpool Scottish at Kemmel in the winter of 1914:

"Just now we have several cripples with an interesting complaint of the feet, brought on my the men having their feet in water and mud for days at a time. The feet are very tender, and the men cannot walk, then when they take their boots off their feet swell like balloons. It is some circulatory trouble, and I think it is the beginning (or threatening stage) of gangrene of the feet which was noticed in the Balkan wars, and which was some of the so-called frostbite in the Crimean War."

Though the definitions were unclear, the result was obvious enough, a steady wastage of men whether they were fighting or not. Nor was there any easy prevention, despite regular foot inspections. One instruction talks of the importance of clean, dry socks: but how this was to be achieved when troops were standing in water was not made clear. Another palliative was covering the feet in whale oil, after the manner of a Channel swimmer, and this may have been partly effective—if not especially pleasant. Gumboots were

Below: **Foot inspection by the Medical Officer of the 12th East Yorkshire regiment in a support trench, near Reclincourt, January 9, 1918.**

Above: **The chess players. German NCOs, including a medic on the left, play behind the lines. In addition to sport and drink, other diversions included reading and music, plus card games—like the German "Skat."**

issued to British troops from 1915, but never to everybody, and definitely not for the attack when they were a hindrance.

Trench foot and frost bite were just two ways of becoming a "non-battle casualty." There were many others, and, as the British official history Medical Services makes clear, as many men were effected by disease, debilitation, and accident as were wounded by the enemy. In hot and disease-ridden areas non-battle casualties actually were several fold greater in number than battle casualties. It was true, however, that disease and other ailments were much less likely to be fatal. Somewhere between two and ten percent of battle casualties admitted to a medical unit later died, while deaths through sickness, even in the most unhealthy East African theater, would never exceed three percent.

Nevertheless non-battle casualties were filling many hospital beds throughout the war. On the Western Front gastric problems, respiratory diseases, influenza, and accident all bulked large, and were doubtless symptomatic of the conditions in the trenches. As Ernest Parker serving

with the Durham Light Infantry recalled, boils and diarrhea were the far from pleasant result of drinking boiled shell hole water when fresh was unavailable. There were also a myriad more exotic illnesses that claimed smaller numbers of men. Tuberculosis, mumps, and scarlet fever were just some of these. Venereal diseases, gonorrhea, syphilis, and others, led to 150,000 hospital admissions—and the greatest number of cases were contracted in France where brothels were legion. Robert Graves, then an officer with the Royal Welch Fusiliers, recalled how a batch of ten of his colleagues, felt themselves obliged to be "roistering blades" as new officers:

"Three of them got venereal disease at the Rouen Blue Lamp. They were strictly brought up Welsh boys of the professional classes, had never hitherto visited a brothel, and knew nothing of prophylactics. One of them shared a hut with me. He came in very late and very drunk one night from the Drapeau Blanc and began telling me about his experiences... There were no restraints in France; these boys had money to spend and knew that they stood a good chance of being killed within a few weeks anyhow. They did not want to die virgins. The Drapeau Blanc saved the lives of scores by incapacitating them for future trench service. Base venereal hospitals were always crowded. The troops took a lewd delight in exaggerating the proportion of army chaplains to combatant officers treated there."

The whole issue was a considerable moral dilemma to the authorities, for to suggest precautions was to condone the sexual activity that spread the disease. As the official history somewhat-pompously put it, the answer was both moral persuasion and "preventative outfits." The typical picture seemed to suggest that:

"The weaker a man's nature, the greater is his tendency to rely on outside influences. Left to his own resources at any time he is miserable, but combined with the sudden transition from trench life to comparative freedom he finds himself helpless to direct his own energies along right channels and becomes an easy prey to the ills that attend this frame of mind. The efforts to attract officers and men to pleasing and health-giving recreation huts, fields of sport, and places of healthy amusement during their hours off duty or during leave in a modern town should be redoubled… Should these efforts fail and the risk of infection be run, the sufferer should be encouraged to report to an early treatment center."

Some of the "ills" spoken of were doubtless occasioned by lack of wife or regular girl friend—and being cut off from home.

In an age before the general use of telephones, letter writing had a disproportionate importance in the life of the trench dwellers. With leave irregular, or nonexistent, over a period of months or years, letters were the one real contact with

Below: **German letter writers at work in a trench. This particular illustration was itself sent as a postcard by Wilhelm Meyer, an NCO of the 39th Ersatz Battalion, 10th Ersatz Division "in the West."**

Deutscher Mut und deutsches Erbarmen
gehen siegreich Hand in Hand!

Above: **"German courage and German compassion go triumphant hand in hand!"** The propaganda message on a field postcard of IV Reserve Corps, which also thanked Fraulein Elli Rothinger for sending cigarettes to Paul, her soldier boyfriend.

home. The most literate were the most lucky, but even those who were unable to read and write would sometimes get others to send letters for them. Even so, this was seldom a pure form of self-expression or open communication. Letters had to be censored, and sensitive detail about times, units, and places had to be omitted. There was also plenty of information that most soldiers would rather their nearest and dearest did not know. Hal Kerridge, serving with the Gordons, noticed that the men soon got used to writing in an "innocuous style"—thus preventing parents from becoming more miserable than they already were. Tommy was always "in the pink," or "quite well," or "looking forward to seeing you"—seldom, if ever, feverish, scared, or exhausted.

One unspoken rule operated in communicating with home. This was that where loved ones had been killed at the front, friends and officers writing home would always say that they had

Above: **Postman of 4th (Territorial) Battalion The Duke of Wellington's (West Riding Regiment). The Royal Engineers Army Postal Service was responsible for getting mail to units, which then distributed it further.**

Left: "For love and Fatherland!" One of hundreds of patriotic postcards produced on both sides. This particular example was sent in April, 1916, by "Anna" to her dear brother, a soldier in the 9th Bavarian Infantry.

Below: French postcard of 1914 showing a German laden with loot, blown down by a highlander.

P'feu !.......

Above: **Romanticized war—nevertheless many liaisons were formed in the face of a highly uncertain future.**

Above: **French postcard cartoon of a Bavarian Landsturm infantryman, 1914.**

been killed "instantly"—or for sake of variety "painlessly," or "heroically." Any hint of suffering to the relatives of the deceased was strictly taboo. Here, just one such short but typical missive of bad tidings must stand in for the hundreds of thousands:

13th Battalion, King's Liverpool Regiment B.E.F.

Dear Mrs Gill,

I very much regret to state that your husband No. 42725 Private RF Gill was killed in action on the night of September 24th. He suffered no pain, being killed instantly by a shell, he is buried in a cemetery behind the line. His loss is greatly felt throughout the platoon, for he was such a jolly fellow and an excellent soldier. Please accept our deepest sympathy in your great loss.

Yours Faithfully,

J. Corrigan, 2nd Lieutenant, Officer Commanding 13th Platoon.

At 39, Alice's husband, the jolly Private Gill, of Upper Aughton Road, Birkdale, Southport, had been a relatively old soldier. He still lies in a well-tended grave "behind the line" at the Dozinghem military cemetery, near Poperinge. Interestingly the very name of the cemetery is itself a joke, which might have appealed to his sense of humor. It takes its title from one of three casualty clearing stations in this area set up in preparation for the third battle of Ypres—Mendinghem, Dozinghem, and Bandaghem.

Another sort of commonplace note or letter was the one which men hoped would never be read: the last letter for wife or family. Some left them at home, others carried them around or wrote them afresh at the start of a new offensive. Many were very simple: for some a note in the pay book which left "all to mother," passed for a last will and testament. Others were longer, more personal. Occasionally, pomposity or patriotism took center stage. In light of his later attitude to the way the war was fought, and to the enemy, the tone of the "last letter" of Lieutenant Basil Liddle Hart of the King's Own Yorkshire Light Infantry makes interesting reading:

> "In the event of my death on active service. It is my wish that you do not wear mourning and that if any flowers are used, that they shall be white roses. If you desire to put up any memorial whatsoever, it is my express wish that it take the form of an endowed cot at a hospital, preferably military. I do not wish you to regard my death as an occasion for grief, but one for thanksgiving, for no man could desire a nobler end than to die for his country and the cause of civilization. A short life which finishes nobly is surely far better than to drag out an ignominious existence. My one hope is to be united to you in the next life. Finally to misquote Dickens, 'It is a far, far better thing that I do, than I have ever done, or ever should have done.'"

Fortunately for him the letter was not needed. For everyone else it would perhaps have been interesting to know what would have happened had one of the self-proclaimed innovators of Blitzkrieg been killed in 1916, before he was able to expound his ideas.

One of the most evocative descriptions of the fully-developed trench system at night came from the pen of Royal Fusiler officer Christopher Stone, at Cambrin in December 1917:

> "I have just come in from a tour of the firing line. It would interest you as an experience: but I suppose it shall soon bore me to death. I have on my new, long waders, thigh gumboots and a mackintosh and my india rubber gloves, so am quite proof against the mud. It's a lovely, warm night with a bit of moonlight; light enough to see your way without a torch. Most of the trenches have footboards laid down in them which keeps them fairly clean but greasy. I go up a communication trench first of all, up the centre of our section and pass "C" Company Headquarters where Black is asleep. Macdougall is said to be out in front by himself examining the wire. I go on to the fire trenches and

Below: **Battle of Thiepval Ridge, September, 1916: Stretcher bearers carry a wounded man over the top of a trench.**

then turn right-handed. It's all zig-zag work of course: a bay and then a traverse, a bay then a traverse, endlessly from the North Sea to the Swiss frontier without a break! In about every third bay there are two sentries standing on the firestep and looking out over the parapet. At the corners of the bays there are often glowing braziers and men sleeping round them or half asleep: and you pass the entrance to dugouts and hear men murmuring inside, and the hot charcoal fumes come out. On and on: sometimes I clamber up beside the sentries and look out. There's little to see, rough ground, the barbed wire entanglement about 15 yards away, the vague line of the German trenches. If a flare goes up it lights the whole place for 30 seconds and is generally followed by a good deal of rifle fire. You see the flash at the muzzle of the rifle. If you hear a machine gun you duck your head. The bullets patter along the parapet when they do what they call traversing: backwards and forwards they patter—quite a sensation."

One significant problem of living in the trenches was that very often one fire bay or communication trench would look very much like another. Orientation could be fraught with hazard—and the soldiers' memoirs abound with working parties or reliefs that became hopelessly lost. With the usual landmarks like churches, woods, and houses obliterated, directions could take on a highly surreal quality. The lost were told, for example, "to turn left at the foot sticking out of the parapet, watch out for motor car corner, then left at the dead horse." In very bad conditions, particularly at night, speeds might not be measured not in miles per hour, but hours per mile. For this reason, the work of the Royal Engineers and their opposite numbers, in producing up-to-date trench maps was vital. Though there were false starts, such as the diabolically misleading series of sheets produced in early 1915 in which the top of the map was not north but the enemy line, progress was considerable.

Below: **Aerial view of trenches near Cambrai. A clear view of the trench system plan emerges: the shadow lines are belts of wire, the crenellated lines are the fire and support lines, the zig-zags are communication trenches.**

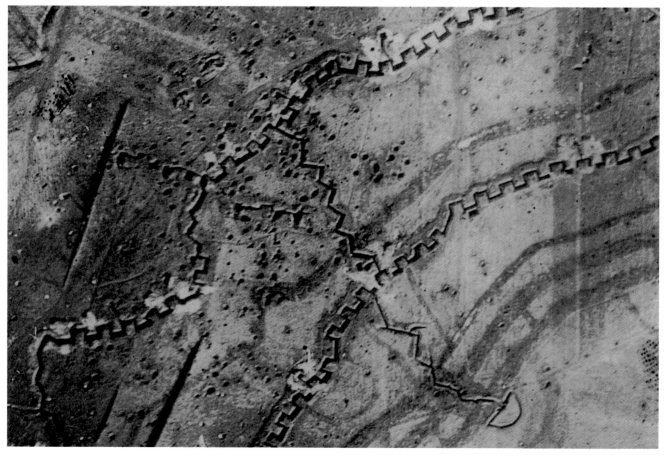

Above: **What was once a tolerably thick woodland—just one part of the Franco-German border turned to moonscape.**

Naming trenches and strong points was also helpful. In places, the designations bespoke either rampant homesickness, or vivid imaginations. East of Delville Wood on the Somme the British names for the German trenches were inspired by the tap room. About half a mile in front of Ginchy was Porter Trench which came to a junction with Pilsen Lane, near Beer Trench. Hop and Ale were nearby communication trenches. The non-alcoholic Tea and Cocoa trenches were north of the wood.

Within Delville Wood itself there was another strange logic to the names of the rides between the trees. Those going north were named for London thoroughfares, while Edinburgh streets ran south. Some names, like Lancashire Sap and Munster Alley, were essentially badges of regimental ownership. Others were descriptive, hence the Elbow and the Wonder Work. Around Houplines the flavor was rustic with names like Quality Street, Haystack Farm, and Dairy Lane. Near Hill 13 and the Bethune Road, a more analytical mind gave names beginning with "B" to all the trenches.

Keeping the trenches supplied was a major undertaking, as Lieutenant John Reith of 5th Battalion of the Cameronians recorded:

"As Transport Officer to the 19th Brigade I began to think I was of some importance to the war. I supplied the trenches with a new form of concertina, barbed wire entanglement and handled also the first consignment of steel loophole plates for the use of snipers ... very useful things once they were properly camouflaged. The usual stores included dug-out frames, hurdles, sandbags by the thousand, duck walks, and timber of all sizes."

Private George Brame of 2/5th Battalion, East Lancashire Regiment, was employed on a working party at just one of many trench stores dumps, near Fresnoy. Though the work was preferable to being in the trenches the amount of material flowing to the front was incredible. His Sergeant offered the very believable calculation that £30,000 of stores was moving through this dump alone every week. As Brame spent three months here, he was in no way surprised that the war was costing millions a day.

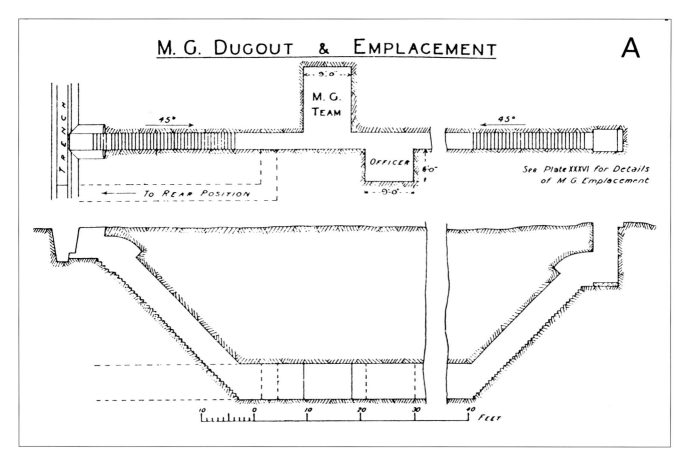

M. G. DUGOUT & EMPLACEMENT

A

M.G. Team

OFFICER

TRENCH

45°

45°

To Rear Position

See Plate XXXVI for Details of M G Emplacement

9'·0"

9'·0"

6'·0"

FEET

Left: Diagram of an entrenched British machine gun post, showing how ideally the position could be reached by a tunnel from the main trench line. The machine gunners and the officer have separate, deep cover dug-outs.

Nevertheless if Brame had had access to the official statistics, he would still have been impressed. The supply of timber "for war requirements" needed a committee to itself, and while Britain's biggest quantity of wood still went to the collieries, government needs in 1918 would peak at 165,920,040 cubic feet of sawn timber. In France at this time, 11,500 Canadian lumberjacks with 7,766 laborers were hacking at the forests. In 1917, efforts were made to supplement the soldiers meat ration with rabbit—successfully, as was evidenced by the five million leftover skins. This led to the establishment of perhaps the war's most bizarre body, the "Army Rabbit Skin Clearing Committee"—which handled a healthy return. The rabbits were however dwarfed by the clothing mountains. Orders included, over the duration, and among many other things, 137 million pairs of worsted socks, 45 million pairs of ankle boots, 15 million pairs of short cotton drawers, and 54 million flannel shirts. At the end of the war the leftover garments were sold by the ton. Things got really serious when it came to ammunition supply. Very rough calculation shows a British production of 220 million shells, 100 million hand grenades, and 8,637,112,000 bullets.

Some of the most heartfelt British anecdotes surrounded the supply of rum to the trenches. This came up in small stoneware jars marked "SRD." There were many humorous interpretations of this inscription including "Service Rum Diluted" and "Seldom Reaches Destination." A number of historians, who should know better, have accepted the more plausible of Tommy's jokes as fact. The actual, and rather mundane explanation of the lettering was "Supply Reserve Depot"—which is where the containers were returned. Though we are now aware that alcohol

Left: German officers and non-commissioned officers around the Christmas tree in a comfortable billet at Lorgies, 1914.

does not warm the body, the tot of rum was embraced by the vast majority of the men as a welcome morale booster. Some men, otherwise teetotal, drank the trench rum. The bearers of the precious liquid were frequently viewed with suspicion—it was never certain that it would not be drunk on the way, or otherwise "lost." In many units doling out the rum became something of a ceremony, with a junior officer supervising the NCO with the rum jar.

The officers' own tastes were likely to be more refined. In some of the top class regiments French champagne did actually make it to the front on rare occasion, but the tipple of choice was usually whiskey. Christopher Stone wrote, with only moderate exaggeration, that whiskey shortages were potentially desperate:

"As the Doctor says, under modern conditions the supply of whiskey is as vitally necessary as that of shells. It is a fact that about 50 percent of the officers, probably more, cannot keep going even in normal trench warfare without alcohol of some sort, and in a fight we all need it."

Though full-blown alcoholism does appear in the British medical history as a cause of "non-battle casualty" it is surprising how very few went this way. Doubtless it was difficult for the budding dipsomaniac to get enough drink to feed his habit in the front line, but it was probably also the case that drunks were among the first to take stupid risks, have accidents, or fail to take cover under fire. What else was kept in the front line trenches could be more surprising than the relatively modest supplies of drink. A list of booty from the German trenches at Beaumont Hamel, taken in November 1916, includes, as one might expect, some thousands of rounds of ammunition, gas cylinders, grenades, and other paraphernalia of war. Less predictable were the Norwegian Sardines, 56 iron kegs—contents unknown, Cat o' nine tails, bottled lager, piano, dancing slippers, and a quantity of "women's clothing."

That men could survive so long in such apparently impossible conditions was remarkable. For many the decider between continuing discipline and fortitude on the one hand, and total collapse on the other, was the hope that they would last

Above: **Men of the Loyal North Lancashire Regiment outside their billet. By the improvised washing line of drying socks, an unknown hand has scrawled "SUVLA." The 6th Battalion of the regiment had been in Gallipoli.**

long enough to be moved on, or back to somewhere more hospitable. Indeed it is difficult to overstate how important the rotation of troops was in making trench warfare possible. Though there were instances, particularly early on, where units spent long periods in the front line, a lifesaver for so many was the various methods whereby units would be cycled in and out of the trenches. As used by the French the so called "Noria" or "bucket" system was a key to long-term survival, and has been credited with particular success at Verdun. As an American correspondent recorded:

> "The one sight of the battle at Verdun that will always live in my memory is that of the snow-covered and ice-coated road north of Bar-le-Duc constantly filled with two columns of trucks. Some were moving north, the others south, and their swaying and lurching progression was comparable to that of young elephants. It was well nigh impossible to drive on that icy road."

According to one calculation, vehicles were passing up the "Sacred Way" one every 14 seconds day and night. For the drivers, 15 hour shifts were commonplace with longer demanded in times of emergency. Columns of men on foot, which another eye witness found difficult to distinguish from "lumps of mud," the color of the brown Verdun clay, were almost equally numerous. The overall result, achieved so laboriously, was that a majority of the French army passed through Verdun. So it was that the death and privations were shared round among the infantry with rough equality, preventing dangerous breakdowns.

In the British systems it became usual to keep only one, or at most two, battalions of a brigade in the front line: the others would be further back in "support" or rest. These terms were relative as support areas might well be subject to shelling, and working parties had a nasty habit of catching up with the under-employed. But being out of the eye of the storm could have a remarkable, if

Left: British troops try and
snatch some rest in the
Somme trenches.

Below: The 129th Baluchis
near Messines. At various
times troops from all
corners of the British
and French Empires
would serve on the
Western Front.

Above: **The British advance near Morval, supporting the XIV Corps attack, September 25, 1916.**

ultimately temporary, restorative quality. Those units at the front, divided down into companies, so that only part of each battalion occupied the most dangerous places at any given moment. The records of various of the battalions of 8th Division speak of stints in the very front line trenches as short as four days in good times. Around Ypres in the spring of 1916, Henry Dundas, an officer with the Scots Guards, described how the Guards brigades adopted a series of eight and 16-day stints, relieving one another on the front lines in turn. There were still several thousand casualties, but these were spread over all the battalions, and at least some of the troops were rested at any given moment. Dundas actually found time for cricket when out of the line. The main drawback from his perspective seemed to be that he always returned to a different sector: "and so I started all square as regards going into a new line."

Beyond the front line trench lay an even more exotic and dangerous place. No man's land was rarely visited by the living, unless one was on a wiring party or patrol, and even then it was not usually in daylight. Yet here were to be found some of the worst horrors, as was discovered by Norman Collins when acting as officer to a burial party at Beaumont Hamel in November 1916. The first of the dead were Seaforths, who were sometimes the brothers or cousins of the men collecting them. Later he was finding Newfoundlanders who had been killed on July 1, collecting paybooks and personal items before shovelling the dead into waterlogged shell holes. Much of the flesh was missing from their faces, but they still smelt, though "not as repulsive as one might suppose." So far so good, but there was more to follow:

"The dead Newfoundlanders looked very ragged, and the rats were running out of their chests. The rats were getting out of the rain of course, because the cloth over the rib cage made quite a nice nest . . . when you touched a body, the rats just poured out from the front. . . To think that a human being provided a nest for a rat was a pretty dreadful feeling. The puttees on the men's legs looked quite round but when the flesh goes from under the puttee, there is just a bone and if you stand on it, it just squashes. . . you never forget it." Hunting rats with trench clubs, revolvers, pet dogs, bayonets, and poisons became a staple of the soldiers' memoirs of the trench war. Perhaps the most final solution was that used by some of the South African troops. At night they would lay a rifle on top of the trench, bayonet fixed, with a tempting piece of cheese skewered on the point. As soon as the scurrying coincided with the position of the cheese the trigger was pulled—with what one man described as "wonderful results."

Nightmare situations were by no means limited to rats, nor the Allied dead. Lieutenant Edwin Vaughan of the Warwickshire's made a particularly horrible discovery in April 1917.

"At the Epéhy crossroads we found a huge cat squatting on the chest of a dead German, eating his face. It made us sick to see it, and I sent two men to chase it away. As they approached it sprang snarling at them, but they beat it down with their rifles. . ."

Dead bodies became a familiar feature of a grim landscape. Yet the dead were not bad news to all. Frederick Hodges of the Lancashire Fusiliers was just one of many to notice that the pockets of the dead were usually empty and hanging out: looters were frequently on the scene before the burial parties. Some souvenir hunting was official—shoulder straps and documents were destined for the edification of intelligence officers, and the taking of caps and helmets was commonly winked at. The majority of the efforts were however strictly private enterprise: soldiers would be seen wearing several watches, or with rings and razors appropriated from the dead.

It was raiding parties and patrols that visited no man's land more often than any others. At

Below: **The stark reality of war; dead Germans in a trench during the Battle of Ypres, July 31, 1917.**

times of intense activity, patrols could be virtually a nightly activity: German soldier Martin Müller led just one of the many of March 1916:

"About a quarter to eight we started—Strauss and Private Tschoppe with me...The distance between the trenches at this point was about 120 yards. The ground was perfectly flat and bare, so afforded but little cover. We scrambled over our own wire and then crawled noiselessly over the thin grass which covered the ground. I was in front with the two others behind me, in a sort of wedge. The stars were not yet out and the night consequently rather dark. From the enemy came the usual occasional shots, sometimes interspersed with the rattle of a machine gun. Now and then a bullet whistled over us, but without troubling us, for here the trenches on both sides are built up above the level of the ground, and shots, being generally aimed at the parapet, don't often strike the earth between the lines. Our side, having been warned about the patrol, were naturally firing seldom, and always high.

"We advanced very slowly, as the enemy kept sending up star shells, and then we had to remain absolutely motionless. It is not easy either to get along, crawling on the ground, and anyhow it is extremely tiring. Now we can see the flashes from the barrels of the enemy rifles. Tack, tack, tack, tack!... There stood an enemy machine gun, easily recognizable by the faint flash accompanying each shot. Suddenly from the left a narrow but brilliant beam of light pierced the darkness. Apparently the light from a dugout as the door opened for a moment... Then suddenly, half left of us, we heard them starting work on the wire! That was the spot we were making for. So now our job began: we had to find out whether the enemy was removing the wire or mending the gaps. So we crept nearer... I could still see that a shining new wire was being stretched... Our task was accomplished. We could get back. I made a sign to the others; they crawled up to me and I was just going to tell them the result of my observations when Tschoppe, who was close to me on the right, screamed out loud. A bad body wound ! We two others picked him up as carefully as we could and crept a little way back with him. A few bullets struck the soft ground close to us..."

Early acts of bravado, hatched by junior officers or even individuals, gradually gave way to a far more systematized regime initiated and supported at the highest level. Patrols were recognized as a way to glean intelligence, obtain dominance over no man's land, and to degrade the morale and numbers of the enemy in the opposing line.

By 1917, British patrolling methods were much refined, being described in the manual *Scouting and Patrolling* that December. Patrols were to be highly organized, so as to give as many men as possible the chance of honing their skills in their execution. The prime objects of night patrols were gaining information; killing, capturing, or harassing the enemy; or to protect a given area. All members of the patrol were to be given a specific object and passwords to get them through their own lines. Nothing was to be taken on patrol which would give any information to the enemy and men were to go lightly-equipped but well-armed. Revolvers were seen as more convenient than rifles, though men being given revolvers were to be expert in their use. Other close quarter weapons deemed useful for patrol were grenades, trench clubs or "knobkerries," and bayonets. The strength of patrols was varied as to the task in hand. Intelligence patrols could be very small; a surprise raid to throw grenades into an enemy post might well consist of five men; a patrol to engage the enemy might typically consist of from eight to 20. Though it was not always possible to maintain a formation it was useful to have one so as to give all-round protection and give the patrol members an idea where to look for each other. It was also handy as a way to help distinguish friend from foe. In the bigger patrols, light machine guns could go forward to provide support. In such cases, the men formed a rough ring, the forward part of which comprised the scouts, while the machine gun and patrol leader were located near the center of the group.

Though shelling, sniping, and patrol activity were all relatively common, full-blown assaults were actually quite a rare feature of trench warfare—and contrary to the general impression accounted for a distinct minority of the time. Many soldiers had tours of duty in the trenches in

Above: **Northumberland Fusiliers return from the line—one with a captured great coat.**

Left: **A fatigue party carrying duckboards over a support line trench at night, Cambrai, January 12, 1917.**

which they would not be put to this ultimate test. Given the relatively high numbers of casualties these big "shows" generated this was fortunate, but no account of the trenches would be complete without an example of the savage confrontations which could and did occur. A particularly confused maelstrom is vividly recorded by Private William R. Dick, 2/6th Battalion, The Gloucestershire Regiment, during a defensive action at La Vacquerie in December 1917:

"I see the wide, dark waste of shell-churned soil, the tattered wire, and, well over, a dark and far flung line of gray clad stormers; behind them others rising fast, apparently springing from the drab earth in knots and groups, spreading out, surging forward.

"Simultaneously from our trench bursts a great roar of fire. I fire with fiercely jerking bolt, round after round merged into the immense noise. The squat Lewis gun is thrust over the parapet by my right shoulder, it leaps into stabbing bursts of sound, that make my deafened ears ring again and again. The rifle spurts hotly, the Lewis gun ejects whirling streams of cartridge cases that heap thickly by my feet. I breathe whiffs of expended gases escaping from the gun.

"I see the first line of attack appear to wither, men reeling, stumbling, disappearing into the blasted contour of the earth. Others, in loose formation, springing swiftly erect, coming grimly forward. With each short rush the rapid rifle fire rises to a crescendo of savage concentration. From the right, but now hardly audible in the stupendous noise, comes the crashing of bombs. In front, before the furious fire, the German rush has died into the earth again.

"We subside quickly below the parapet as some flanking machine guns commence to sweep the trench top. My rifle is hot to the touch. Above, the parapet is flayed by a constant stream of bullets. Following a gaggle of bloody wounded down the

Below: **An officer of the 10th Scottish Rifles leads the way out of a trench, followed by his men, March 3, 1917.**

trench, an officer with a revolver appears.

"He bellows hastily for bombs, and returns again to the right. A few of us are told off to collect all the bombs we can, and we gather armfuls of captured German egg bombs, mixed with the heavy Mills; they are passed up. . . Suddenly, I hear faintly a medley of confused shouts. . . I see the Company Officer's revolver spurt twice. Four or five smashing explosions disrupt the earth of the parapet, one bomb flies over and bursts on the parados. We crouch, wounded and unwounded, and run the gauntlet of the final volley of bombs. . . The man in front has a bomb splinter in his back, the small rent is surrounded by a red stain. His boot heel is torn too and blood oozes out with every step."

As time went on, trench garrisons were spread thinner and over broader and more complex systems. As Norman Collins remarked in November 1916:

"The thing that strikes me most about the trenches is the small number of men holding the line. One can walk for a hundred yards along the front line trench and never see a soul except a single sentry... About nine tenths of the troops out here never see a German."

This thinning was by no means accidental. Early doctrine had it that large numbers of men should occupy the line, and not yield so much as an inch to the opposition. Packed and inflexible trench lines were very expensive to hold. Such trenches were often defended to the last and filled up with men time and time again. When the enemy finally broke through, they would be confronted by a new line dug behind.

Next came the notion, current by early 1915, of two or three lines dug as part of the same system. This spread the enemy barrage, diminishing its effectiveness, and made it possible to lose one line without compromise to the whole. In the

Below: **Men of the King's Own surrounded by ground sheets and 1908 Pattern webbing in a front line trench. The SMLE rifle hanging to the left has a breech cover to keep out the mud.**

face of battles where defenders still suffered pretty well as badly as attackers, due to overcrowding, bombardment, and ill-advised counterattacks, the theory began to change again. Where it was properly conducted trench warfare could now become a "defensive battle" much more injurious to the attacker than the defender. As the German tactician Balck explained in his *Development of Tactics*, the idea was now to let the enemy waste himself against the trench line, "bleeding himself white" in the attempt to break through. On the defender's side machines and material could be substituted for men, with artillery, machine guns, and mortars replacing the continuous lines.

Finally came the concept of zones which did not necessarily involve trenches at all, but networks of machine gun posts, shell holes, and bunkers which would absorb both huge amounts of punishment and the impetus of the enemy advance. As Ernst Jünger noted, the right simile for the new defense was that of a net:

> "... into which the enemy may penetrate here and there, but where he will at once be overwhelmed on all sides by a web of fire."

Flexibility was the keynote of the defense as General Ludendorff would explain in his memoirs:

> "A new system was devised, which, by distribution in depth and the adaption of a loose formation, enabled a more active defense to be maintained. It was, of course, intended that the position should remain in our hands at the end of the battle, but the infantryman need no longer say to himself: 'here I must stand or fall.'"

By mid–1917, the new concepts were widely applied to the German defences, and would play a significant part in slowing up allied attack. At Passchendaele, for example, a classic pattern with a thin "forward zone" occupied the Pilkem Ridge and outer part of the Gheluvelt plateau, while a stronger second line was concealed behind the reverse slope. A third line fronted the Passchendaele position proper. Further back still new "Flanders II" and "Flanders III" defence positions were under construction. Though the Allies were soon aware of the new methods, there were practical problems in applying them to their own lines, which were often already laid out as

Below: **British diagram showing the use of "spider wire." Odd strands and scattered barriers between major belts were hardly visible on reconnaissance photos and were difficult to clear by bombardment.**

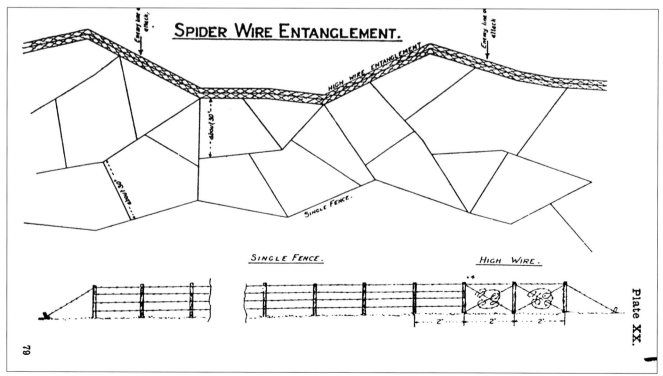

Above: **Part of the town of Armentiers, seen from the air, surrounded by trenches and wrecked by shell fire. Some other places were far worse—being reduced to odd cellars and surface scatterings of bricks.**

lines of trenches, and an understandable reluctance to retreat in order to create the necessary blank canvas.

The advent of the concrete defenses in the middle period of the war has yet to receive anything like its due emphasis. This was particularly significant as structures which could both withstand most shells and provide a nucleus for the defence were a major factor in reducing the numbers needed to hold a position. Though both sides would ultimately use them, it was the Germans who were the pioneers of concrete works. As early as the autumn of 1915, the Dutch press was reporting the ominous news that the Germans were bringing huge barge loads of gravel and basalt down the waterways to the Western Front. This was when the first widespread use of concrete came below ground level to toughen shelters.

As French experiments would demonstrate, though an eight inch shell could penetrate ten feet of soft soil, five feet of concrete was adequate to stop the same projectile. The addition of reinforcement rods made an even more dramatic difference so that just over three feet could prevent penetration. Remarkably, even a monster 15-inch shell could be stopped by just five feet of reinforced concrete. The implications of such calculations in an area like Flanders, where a high water table made digging deep works impossible were considerable, as a report on the German works at Messines observed:

> "The nature of the ground at Messines Ridge, where there is water-bearing sand about 20 feet below the surface, made the construction of deep dugouts there impossible. The mined dugouts that have been found have only 10 to 15 feet of earth cover. For the protection of his men from shell fire the enemy resorted largely to concrete shelters. The roofs of these shelters were originally about, or just about, surface level."

The most effective protection were bunkers in which the mass of concrete exceeded the void

Above: **Allied troops by German bunker, Langemarck. Networks of concrete bunkers revolutionized defense and added a new dimension to the trenchscape.**

within which the troops were ensconced. Australian commentators would note bunkers, amid multiple, overlapping shell holes which suffered only superficial damage. In many instances hits from even large shells only removed a few inches of concrete from the surface.

The pillbox—a small, stand alone fort from which troops could sally, or machine guns could fire in unexpected directions—added another dimension to the war of construction. Concrete mini-fortresses had been observed in the German line by 1916, but it was at Passchendaele in 1917 that their effectiveness would be really proved. As General Gough ruefully observed, the enemy had created a new type of defense system comprising:

"...small but very powerful concrete shelters. These were covered with mud and scattered through the desert of wet shell holes which stretched in every direction. They were impossible to locate from a distance, and in any case were safe against anything but the heaviest shells. The farms, most of them surrounded by very broad wet ditches, or moats, had also been heavily concreted within their shattered walls, every one of these was a fort in itself."

Pillboxes were excellent cover in a barrage, but if not concealed could be bullet and bomb magnets when the attack came. An excellent description of a captured pillbox near Plug Street was given by Royal Engineer Alan Hyder:

"... nearer our lines than the German, half buried by indescribable debris, lay a captured Jerry pillbox. This massive structure, its walls four or five feet high. It had its loophole peering toward the German lines, while its exit stared Berlin-ward... The pillbox with its chattering machine gun mowing down approaching troops, had attracted the attention of many shells, and evidently a German doctor had shared the room with its gun crew, rendering first aid; while many wounded, sheltering in the lee of its concrete walls had been caught by our guns. Outside, a churned-up mixture of limbs, trenching tools, rapidly decaying bodies, fragments of accoutrements, mud, and foul slime. Inside, a welter of what had been, perhaps six men, lying disjointedly in a foot of discolored water."

WEAPONRY AND EQUIPMENT

SMALL ARMS: RIFLES, MACHINE GUNS, AND GRENADES

To a significant extent, the character of the war in the trenches was dependent on the weapons used. It was the lethality of the guns that made showing oneself on the surface impossibly dangerous much of the time and their effects which helped determine the layout of the trenches and dugouts. The main threats to the soldier's continued existence, in order of importance, were the artillery, machine guns and rifles, and grenades. Edged weapons were a negligible consideration. British statistics compiled on a sample of over 200,000 cases admitted to casualty clearing stations showed that 58.5 percent had been wounded by shells and trench mortars; 39 percent by machine gun and rifle bullets; two percent by grenades and just under a third of one percent by bayonets.

The rifle was the one weapon with which every soldier was thoroughly familiar at the outbreak of war, and the rifles of most nations had a basic similarity. They had magazines to hold the cartridges, allowing repeat shots, and were "bolt action" types. This meant that the mechanism had to be worked manually between rounds, a bolt, like a door bolt, being pulled back and pushed home again to load the cartridge. Nevertheless there were significant differences in detail. The German Mauser was notable for its accuracy, and in its basic G98 infantry model for its long length. This was ideal for bayonet fighting but not so handy in a confined space. It was tolerably swift to reload but had only a five round magazine, and a long bolt pull which meant that the rifle had to be clear of the face when reloading. The French Lebel rifle had been a world leader at the time of its introduction, being in the forefront of the development of small bore weapons and smokeless cartridges. By 1914, it was looking distinctly old-fashioned, being hampered by its under the barrel tube magazine which had to be loaded one cartridge at a time.

The quality of the Short Magazine Lee Enfield, and speed and skill of British riflemen in 1914 has often been remarked, but it is apparent that training also played a significant part. As the report of one German prisoner revealed under questioning:

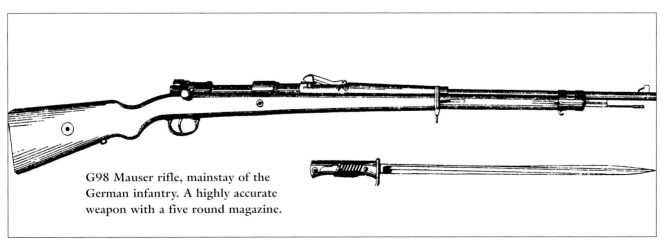

G98 Mauser rifle, mainstay of the German infantry. A highly accurate weapon with a five round magazine.

"When asked if the Germans went in for rapid fire, he replied that only some of their men were practiced, and they only averaged eight to nine rounds per minute. (Their straight bolt is not so easy to work, nor their clip so easy to put in). They do not seem to realize that we train our men to fire 15 well-aimed shots a minute."

Nor was 15 rounds a finite limit: tests had shown that even higher figures could be attained. During an officers' course Lieutenant R. Talbot Kelly of the Royal Artillery noted South African troops who were able to get off 15 shots in rather less than a minute, without loss of accuracy, and most importantly, without taking their eyes from the sights, or stock away from the shoulder. As Ernest Parker of the Durhams, outflanked in a shell hole by German Jäger, with only one comrade to help him, would report:

"I kicked Stone and began firing rapidly over the top of the crater. By the time he had joined me, the dark green figures were drawing level with our position and now they began to falter, falling fast under our enfilading fire. As they worked steadily behind us, each shot winged its man and we kept up the fire until all movement ceased and our ammunition was exhausted. When we looked at the bottom of the shell hole, there were two or three hundred empty cartridge cases under our feet. Not a shot from the German trenches had come in reply, showing plainly that the enemy had retreated from his position of the morning. After we had watched closely for signs of any survivors we began to realize that we had wiped out a whole company…"

The rifleman's weapon was incomplete without its bayonet, designed to be fixed for the final assault with "cold steel." Bayonets were fearsome in appearance, featured significantly in training, and could indeed intimidate an enemy into surrender or flight. But actual injuries were few, as Jean Norton Cru, a veteran of Verdun reported:

"I never saw the bayonet used, never saw the bayonet stained with blood or stuck in a corpse. It was the custom to fix bayonets at the start of an attack; but that was not a reason for calling it a bayonet charge, any more than a charge in puttees."

What was really alarming about the modern magazine rifle, for those who had the wit to see it, was just how efficient a killing machine it could be. By 1914, some had already perceived that closing with enemy troops who were proficient riflemen was going to be a very expensive proceeding. Though there were experiments with spreading troops more thinly, and an acceptance that advances might have to be by bounds covered by other shooters, there was really only one remedy which was generally accepted. This was the bitter pill of attacking more persistently, more aggressively, and with greater determination than the enemy. The French obsession with the attack has been widely noted, but the tactical doctrine of most nations accepted that without attack there could be no success. The *Russian Field Service Regulations* were typical for example when they stated:

"Offensive action is the best method of obtaining our object; only thus can we seize the initiative and force the enemy to do what we wish."

The high casualties of many of the early engagements of the war can be directly traced to such beliefs.

Sniping was a feature of trench warfare from the start, but it was a skill, like so many others, which became more systematized with the passage of time. Nothing was technologically new in sniper equipments, since telescopic sights had existed for about a century by the time war broke out. Nevertheless the methods and scale of use were novel departures. For Herbert McBride, with 21st Battalion of the Canadians, sniping was not so much about accurate shooting as technique, stalking, and moving imperceptibly. Moreover, the equipment for sniping was not just the rifle and scope—difficult to come by in the early days, but reliable ammunition and a telescope for spotting. Lieutenant Cloete gave an admirable description of the usual sniping method:

"The snipers worked in pairs, one observer with a

Right: **Canadian infantry with the short magazine Lee Enfield rifle, March 20, 1916.**

telescope and one with the rifle. They changed over every half hour as it is very tiring to use a telescope for a long period. In action the sniper's job was to work independently and try to pick off any enemy leaders he could see. That was what the Germans did to us and they had no difficulty as we wore officers' uniforms with long tunics, riding breeches, trench boots and Sam Browne belts."

The manuals soon told officers that the best policy was to wear other ranks webbing, carry a rifle, and, if visible at all, try to look just like anyone else. Some took this to heart. Private Fred Hodges was mystified by a public school boy with authority written all over him, who gave out orders to the men round him. Only when he was really close could the pip on the shoulder of the private's uniform be seen and the man be recognized as the platoon officer.

Many just ignored the potentially life-saving advice. Lieutenant John Reith later realized that he made a "pretty conspicuous" figure, being six feet six in his riding breeches and best tunic. Even so, actually being "sniped" came as a completely disorientating shock, which he described as like being hit with a cricket ball:

"But that was not the explanation of the singing in my ears and the crack on the head I had just received. The Germans wouldn't have thrown a cricket ball at me. What could it be? Blast it, I've been hit… Must have been a bullet. Damnation, look at the blood pouring down my new tunic. I've been hit in the head. Has it gone through and smashed up my teeth? No, they were all there. Was the bullet in my head? If so this was the end. Meantime I had better lie down."

He had been hit by a sniper hiding in a brick stack just forty yards away. A sergeant attempted to stop the bleeding using a field dressing, but to no avail. Nevertheless, Reith survived, waking up on a stretcher to discover he had a face wound five inches by three, and "a good bit of bone shot away." The bullet had gone right through, causing a secondary wound to his shoulder.

Good positions to snipe from were also a

Left: **Sniper team from the 4th Royal Berkshires.**

major factor in high tallies and staying alive. In McBride's appreciation there were three main options; sniping posts in and around the main front line; positions a hundred or so yards further back; and the option of crawling out into no man's land to engage the enemy on his own ground. Front line positions were handy, but restricted to whatever field of view your loophole could cover. This could be a useful irritant, forcing the enemy to keep down, but was unlikely to cause many casualties. The alternative of being just behind the front line, gave a better field of fire and allowed a command over a greater section of the front. Crawling out to the enemy was arguably the most deadly method, but could also be the most personally hazardous, as McBride related:

"When it comes to crawling alone out of your own trenches, probably dressed up in one of those 'sniper robes,' I am off that stunt also—by preference, that is—although I have done quite a bit of it. Here, a man is strictly 'on his own' and is apt to be pretty much up against it if anything goes wrong. His field of fire is much limited, no moving about can be indulged in, and generally but one or two shots may be fired before the show is over for the day. Then comes the long, fearful wait until darkness sets in, before the crawl back to your own trenches may be begun."

According to the textbook, two man teams using several positions was the ideal. If one post was compromised they could move to a better spot: the enemy could target one and then find themselves enfiladed from another. Dummy posts would keep the enemy guessing, and might lead to wasted ammunition against unoccupied places. Variety and novelty were prime means of achieving surprise, and some of the ruses employed by snipers have a surprisingly modern feel. Private Fred Wilson of the Manchesters, serving in Gallipoli came upon a badly wounded Turkish sniper at an aid post. Firing from a tree he had accounted for several officers, before he had been located and shot out of his nest. Remarkably, "his face, hands, and arms" were painted green, and he was wearing a "green uniform."

Though sniping was best done in pairs it was

93

perhaps the ultimate personalization of war, with single and individual human targets. This was sometimes difficult to come to terms with: Jack Rogers, a sniper with the Sherwood Foresters, consoled himself that although no stranger to aiming at the heads of his opponents, his purpose was not primarily to kill. The job was equally to prevent activity in the enemy communication trenches, and remind the Germans that you were there. Yet this was an arena where, as McBride put it, a man could really "find himself." Such individuality had not been strictly necessary in the days of shoulder-to-shoulder tactics, but now:

> "...it is pretty much an individual and personal matter, with each soldier working out his own salvation as best he can, for the good of the cause and the preservation of his own hide."

Perhaps this, as much as its "unsporting" nature, made sniping initially unpopular with authority. Not until 1916 was sniping a subject which would be widely and officially taught in recognized Army Schools. Scouting and patrolling were similarly a sort of "madman's land" on the "border of authority," and it was little wonder that for training and organizational purposes these similar skills were often lumped together.

One weapon more than any other conjures up the war in the popular imagination: the machine gun. Even for the infantry, the killing could now be multiple, mechanical, and relatively impersonal. As we have noted, the machine gun was not actually the greatest killer, but it added a diabolical new dimension.

The true machine gun, a weapon which continues to fire automatically as long as a trigger is depressed, had been invented by Hiram Stevens Maxim as long ago as the 1880s. It had seen widespread but small scale use in colonial wars ever since. Yet these conflicts had often been one sided, in the sense that usually only one of the combatants had machine guns, and the results had not been accepted as a measure of what might be expected in European warfare from these weapons of surprise and "opportunity." Perhaps unsurprisingly machine guns were

Left and Right: **Camouflaged and uncamouflaged snipers.**

relatively rare weapons even in 1914. Usually allotted on a scale of two per battalion, there was therefore only about one per five hundred rifles. The realization of the power of the machine gun would lead both to a proliferation of new types, and to a more than a tenfold increase in the ratio of machine weapons to rifles. By the end of the war, every platoon would have some sort of machine gun while separate machine gun companies performed fire missions of their own.

The standard German machine gun of 1914 was the MG 08, a heavy, water-cooled gun set on a steady "sledge" mount. Its bulk and weight were drawbacks, but the mounting could be collapsed to carry like a stretcher, and the water cooling allowed sustained fire without overheating. The ammunition came in 250-round fabric belts, and the cyclic rate was 500 rounds per minute. Commonly, however, fire was slowed to perhaps 50 or 100 rounds per minute, allowing the gun commander to observe the bullet strikes with his binoculars and direct the crew accordingly. Guns were also provided with a magnifying optical sight giving the gunners a better view of the dots on the landscape which were the attacking enemy.

As the compilers of the British publication *Notes From the Front* admitted, the German machine guns were well and imaginatively handled. Sometimes British troops were not aware that the bundle carried like an "African hummock" on the shoulders of the enemy was even a machine gun. At other times sudden surprise bursts would emanate from coppices, bunkers, or haystacks. As Corporal John Lucy noted at La Bassée in October 1914:

"Sergeant Benson came into our trench at a run, saying he had spotted the machine gun in the right haystack and sent a message through to our guns. This was interesting and in a short time our shells arrived and exploded. But they hit the wrong haystack and set it blazing. The machine gun stuttered again and we popped down as the bullets traversed along the trench top.

'Up,' shouted Benson. 'Rapid fire at the haystack.' We fired hard at the stack, and at its top and sides, but with no effect. That gun was well

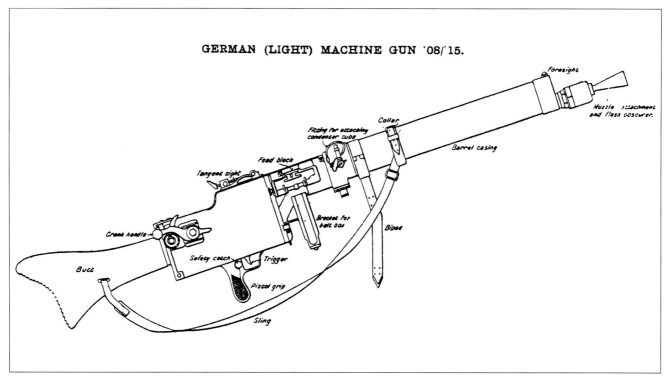

GERMAN (LIGHT) MACHINE GUN '08/15.

Above: Diagram showing the German MG 08/15 light machine gun.

Below: British troops manning a .303 Maxim machine gun, c.1914.

Above: **Machine Gun Corps gunners with the Vickers machine gun, 1916. Both men wear anti-gas "tube" helmets, the gun firer also has the short, padded cape or waistcoat over his uniform for carrying the gun barrel.**

hidden. We learned afterward, too late, that the enemy had the habit of cutting a tunnel from the back right through the center of the haystacks, and mounted their gun in the tunnel; a clever ruse, as no one would fire at the blank center of the stack. Anyway, we failed to put the gun out of action and it killed a good many before we left those trenches."

Though we are perhaps most familiar with descriptions of British Tommies being scythed down by German machine guns, the weapon was no respecter of any nationality. As Colonel G.S. Hutchison of the Machine Gun Corps recalled chillingly of an incident with a Vickers machine gun at High Wood on the Somme:

"With my runner I crept forward among the dead and wounded, and came to one of my guns mounted for action, its team lying dead beside it. I seized the rear leg of the tripod and dragged the gun some yards to where a little cover enabled me to load the belt through the feed block. To the south of the wood Germans could be seen, silhouetted against the sky line, moving forward. I fired at them and watched them fall, chuckling with joy at the technical efficiency of the machine."

The manual writers acknowledged the machine gun gave the concentrated power of 30 or 40 rifles, and what might once have been completely untenable positions were now held successfully.

The British Vickers was similar to its German counterpart, though slightly more modern and moderately lighter. At the end of 1915, these sustained fire weapons were removed from the infantry and redeployed in the machine gun companies of the Machine Gun Corps. Here they were used not only in direct support but to create their own barrages, which could be at targets a mile or more from the gun position, and coordinated with the artillery fire plan. On the Somme, Ernst Jünger vividly recalled being annoyed by "an artist" with a long-range machine gun from which the bullets were dropping almost vertically out of the sky, so as to make taking cover very difficult. In one

Above: **Machine Gun Corps gunners with the Vickers machine gun *c.*1916. Note how the weapon is fitted with both the normal, sustained fire tripod, and a smaller, folded bipod for rapid deployment.**

celebrated example, on August 24, 1916, ten guns of the 100th MG Company fired 975,000 rounds in a barrage in support of an attack. To sustain such an orgy of fire required significant organization, and supplies of water for cooling were a major problem. Into the guns of the 100th went first four petrol cans of water; then all the water bottles of the company; then the "urine tins from the neighborhood." Ammunition moved up in a continuous carrying party, while Private Robertshaw and Artificer Bartlet maintained a belt-filling machine for twelve hours. Unsurprisingly, it is recorded that many of the

company were virtually asleep on their feet when firing ceased.

Perhaps the most important departure as the war progressed was the advent of the "light" machine gun—something which helped make possible very significant changes in the tactics of the trench war. The fact that there were now machine weapons which one man could carry, and if necessary fire by himself, and which could be moved and set up within a few seconds made it possible for infantry to take their own support fire with them pretty much wherever they went. Moreover, it was now realistic to expect infantry to attack machine-gun posts with some chance of success; to economize drastically on men in forward positions and to secure quickly-captured positions with machine guns. There were early experiments with a number of different weapons, including the Danish-designed Madsen gun, but it was the American-designed Lewis, used in large numbers by the British, which had the most widespread impact. As one American reporter was moved to observe in 1916:

> "Nothing the whole war has brought out has been of so much real use to the British Army as the Lewis machine gun. It has done wonders. It has almost countered the British aversion to tactics."

The Lewis appeared strangely impractical: it had an industrial air, looking thick barreled and ungainly, with a less-than-elegant 47-round ammunition pan perched on the top. To the untutored eye it was neither rifle nor machine gun, but then this was the secret of its success.

The thick barrel was really no such thing, being an ordinary air-cooled rifle type barrel shrouded in cooling fins and an external cover. The whole thing weighed about 26lb—and though this still required strength and stamina to tote effectively, the weight was but a third or less of a tripod mounted water-cooled gun.

Some minor reliability problems aside, the only real drawbacks to the Lewis were two: its inability to provide sustained fire over long periods, and its limited long range accuracy given that it was intended to be fired primarily from a bipod. In these two areas the Vickers remained unsurpassed, but by fitting the weapons into their respective tactical niches, the best of both worlds was almost obtained. Lewis guns were used right at the sharp end, carried forward with the infantry platoons, fired from shell holes in no man's land, and redeployed rapidly from place to place. The Vickers was kept further back, in second or support lines.

Below: **Madsen Light Machine Gun, seen here with British troops. The Danish-designed Madsen, with its distinctive curved magazine, was one of the first light machine guns to be used as a mobile infantry weapon.**

As production of the Lewis gun increased through 1915, it proved possible to equip at least one section of each infantry platoon. With its other sections composed of riflemen and bombers, the platoon began to achieve considerable tactical flexibility in its own right. The appearance of the Lewis was a serious worry to the Germans, with the result that there were parallel developments on the enemy side of the line. By adapting and lightening the MG 08, it proved possible to make a reliable German bipod mounted weapon. But the MG 08/15, as the new gun was known, was never a match for the Lewis. It appeared relatively late in the day, and retained the water-cooling of its predecessor. Though effective enough, it weighed about 40lb when a 100-round belt of ammunition and the water were included. The German "light" machine gun was therefore at the very limit of what could be carried—even so about 130,000 were produced and the MG 08/15 did murderous work on many occasions.

The French were very interested in the concept of "walking fire," the idea of a machine gun which could be carried forward with the infantry, and where possible actually fired on the move—thereby obviating stalled attacks. The real problem was that until late 1915 there was no weapon available in any quantity with which this was a realistic possibility. When the Chauchat model 1915 was developed there were therefore high hopes. Here at last appeared to be a modern gun with full automatic capability, having a handy, detachable 20-round magazine, weighing only 21lb. On the face of it, this specification should have made the Chauchat even better than the Lewis, and the Americans also adopted the Chauchat when they entered the war. The reality

Left: **British officer cadets with a Lewis gun, seen here on a tripod. Later it would be usual for the Lewis to be used in a more mobile role from a bipod.**

Below: **The appearance of the highly portable, American-designed Lewis Gun was a worrying development for the Germans, who set about designing their own equivalent.**

was a sad disappointment. Poor ergonomics made the Chauchat difficult to use, and any carelessness was rewarded with a smack in the face from the recoil. If anything, the weapons used by the Americans were worse still, with many mechanical malfunctions to add to the existing tales of woe. Yet, whatever their relative shortcomings, the MG 08/15 and the Chauchat helped make possible similar tactical advances to those pioneered with the Lewis.

The grenade was one of the unexpected stars of the trench war. Widely neglected in 1914, it was seen primarily as something that engineers might use in a siege. Moreover, many of the bombs that did exist at the time were pretty primitive affairs—French and German ball grenades filled with black powder, and some means of ignition such as a friction pull. There were a few exceptions. The British had a complex "No. 1" stick grenade with a brass head and trailing streamer designed to explode on impact. It may have been sophisticated, but it was expensive and only made in tiny numbers. More worryingly, it had such a long handle that a throw from inside a trench could result in the grenade striking the wall and exploding prematurely.

Nevertheless the grenade was quickly recognized as the one thing which gave the soldier anything like a chance against an enemy in a trench. Even if the target was invisible the grenade could be lobbed over, and an explosion in a confined space could be devastating. The shortage of grenades which occurred in late 1914 and 1915 was every bit as bad as the shortage of shells. Yet where shells were impossible to improvise, it did prove possible to make primitive explosive devices to throw at the enemy. The result was the advent of such alarming devices as the "Jam Tin" and the "Racquet Bomb." Home factories also began to manufacture simple stop gaps—often cans full of explosive with fuses sticking out of the top which were lit by banging down, rubbing on a brassard, or lighting with a match or pipe. Ernst Jünger describes German troops at Lens, who always kept a cigar alight, for:

Left: French soldier from the 10th Army holding a Chauchat light machine gun with semi-circular magazines, August 25, 1916.

Left: **Realistic "bombing" practice. Note how one man is throwing a bomb over the traverse, while one or more men, just visible to the thower's left, are ready to round the corner.**

Below: **The British "Pitcher" hand grenade. One of the "emergency" models introduced early in the war. The user removed the cap and used it to pull the cord to ignite the fuse: accidents were frequent with this type.**

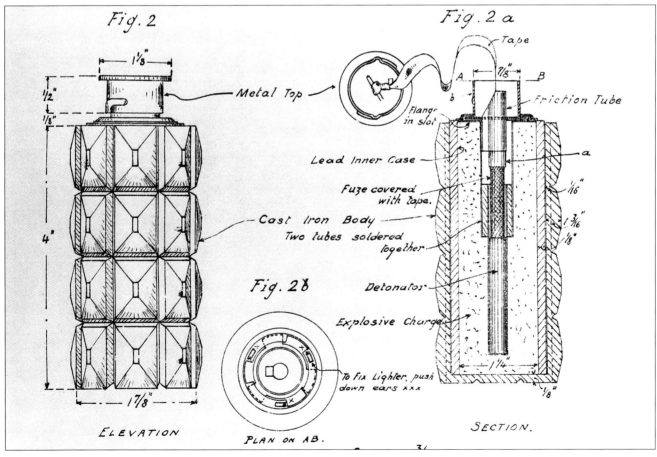

Fig. 2

Fig. 2 a

Fig. 2b

Metal Top

Tape

Flange in slot

Friction Tube

Lead Inner Case

Fuze covered with tape.

Cast Iron Body
Two tubes soldered together

Detonator

Explosive Charge

To Fix Lighter, push down ears xxx

ELEVATION

PLAN ON AB.

SECTION.

"...at the time we had no bombs with pull out fuses. There was merely a bit of fuse sticking out and one held it to the cigar before throwing... They were tin boxes with a handle filled with explosive, old nails, and scrap iron. They were heavy and unwieldy, but effective."

As 1915 progressed, new and more reliable types of grenade appeared. Significant among these were the German stick grenade and the British Mills bomb; both effective, but very different devices.

The German stick grenade consisted of a wooden handle with a steel cylinder full of explosive on the end. A cord passed through the handle and up to a friction device, which was itself linked to a fuse and detonator. A sharp pull on the cord caused the friction device to activate, not unlike the pull of a Christmas cracker—and this in turn lit the fuse. The grenade was now thrown. The fuse burned for five and a half seconds before the detonator acted, and the grenade exploded. The cylinder had a relatively thin sheet construction, so the main effect from the German stick bomb was its blast. This made it quite suitable for use in the attack, when the thrower could be reasonably confident he would not be hit by fragments from his own bomb. It was also very good to throw into trenches and bunkers.

The Mills bomb, so named after the inventor, was a relatively heavy cast metal ovoid, within which was a spring-loaded striker. The user pulled a pin which released the lever, but the bomb remained safe until thrown, when the lever sprang off and the striker banged down on a percussion cap which lit the fuse. A few seconds later the fuse reached the detonator and the bomb went off in a cloud of whirring metal fragments. This fragmentation effect made the

Below: **A German sentry armed with a "potato masher" hand grenade keeps watch from the trenches with a periscope, 1916.**

Above: **The British No. 5 grenade or "Mills bomb:"**
handy and highly lethal, one of the most successful
grenades of the war.

"...we suddenly came on a German sap 15 yards away. The first thing I knew about it was a rifle going off point blank and I turned round and cursed the sniper who was with me as I thought he had let off his rifle. As I turned I saw the earth at his feet kick up and then a bullet came at my feet and I looked and saw the Huns within a handshake distance firing. Luckily they were either so flurried or such putrid shots that they did not hit us—anyway I was in a shell hole almost instantaneously. But the second I got in, I saw a hand grenade just falling in my hole so I dashed off and got into another five yards further away. As I ran they threw six at me which burst in a shower all round and I felt my left hand go numb as I fell into the crater and when I looked there was only a red pulp with splinters of bones and tendons in it on the end of my arm. They threw some more but did not land in my shell hole luckily. The first thing I decided was that my only chance of not being captured was to stay till night then try to crawl back before they came out and got me. Then I got out my field dressing and poured the iodine over the jelly and put on the dressings as well as I could and then

Mills particularly powerful, but not particularly suitable to use at close quarters in the open—ideally it was thrown from cover, or when the thrower was able to get himself flat when throwing. This made the Mills an ideal defensive bomb. Moreover, though there were accidents, the Mills was far safer and far more reliable than the myriad devices that preceded it. Indeed, once the Mills bomb was generally available, it became common practice to divide British grenades into "first class" bombs and others. Generally the Mills fulfilled the first category. Usually British troops were issued with two Mills bombs before any offensive action, with dedicated bombers having a canvas bucket or waistcoat to carry greater numbers.

One account of being hit with a grenade must suffice for the thousands of such incidents that occurred. Lieutenant N.V.H. Symons of the Worcestershires was out in no man's land placing snipers in October 1917 when:

Above: **A Belgian grenadier demonstrates the throwing of**
a Mills bomb.

bound my arm to my stick with my tie. As soon as this was done I ate my maps with all the HQs etc. marked on them and also pages out of my note book with invaluable information on them. . ."

As early as the beginning of 1915, it was well appreciated that head on linear attacks against trenches were hugely costly. A far better way to clear a section of trench was to approach it as a small, fast-moving group, enter the enemy line at a point, then bomb along it throwing grenades over the intervening traverses. Any who resisted would be tackled at close quarters with bayonets, trench clubs, pistols, and entrenching tools. The German "shock" troops, and British Grenadier Parties using these tactics pointed the way—however dimly—toward completely new infantry tactics. Platoons armed with the full gamut of weapons, including light machine guns, would attack as loose gaggles—rushing from cover to cover, firing to protect those advancing.

The grenade duel became a brutal and enduring feature of trench combat. A particularly dramatic example was recorded by Ernst Jünger at Cambrai, when, following a reckless drive through a trench block set up between British and German trenches, a full-scale bomb battle broke out:

"We were all wrought up and, snatching up bombs, ran to take part in the improvised assault... The Commanding Officer himself, Captain von Brixen, was among the foremost. He picked up a rifle, and he shot down several enemy bombers over our heads. The English resisted valiantly. Every traverse was contested. Mills bombs and stick bombs crossed and recrossed. Behind each we found dead or still quivering bodies. We killed each other out of sight; and there were losses on our side too. A bomb fell close to the orderly and burst before he could get clear. He fell with a dozen wounds, from which his blood trickled into the soil. We sprang over his body. Thunderous reports gave us our direction. Hundreds of eyes lay in wait in the desolation... Each time that one of the egg-shaped bombs appeared, the eye seized it with a precision only possible to a man whose life hangs on the

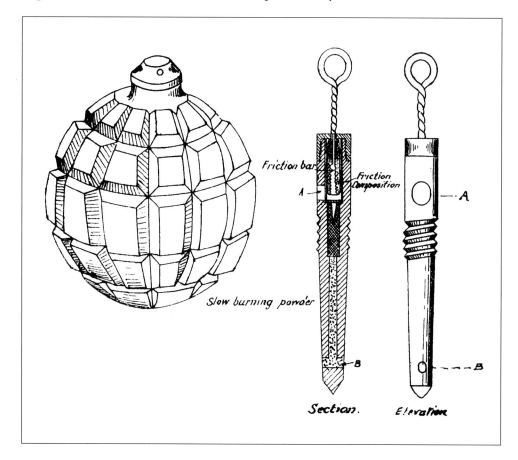

Friction bar

Friction Composition

A — — A

Slow burning powder

— B — — B

Section. Elevation.

Left: **Diagram of the 1913 model German "Kugel" or ball hand grenade. A relatively low technology weapon, it was lit by means of a friction pull. Nevertheless it caused vicious metal fragments and was particularly effective when used defensively from cover.**

Right: **British map of German trenches and defences around Ypres, dated August 15, 1917.**

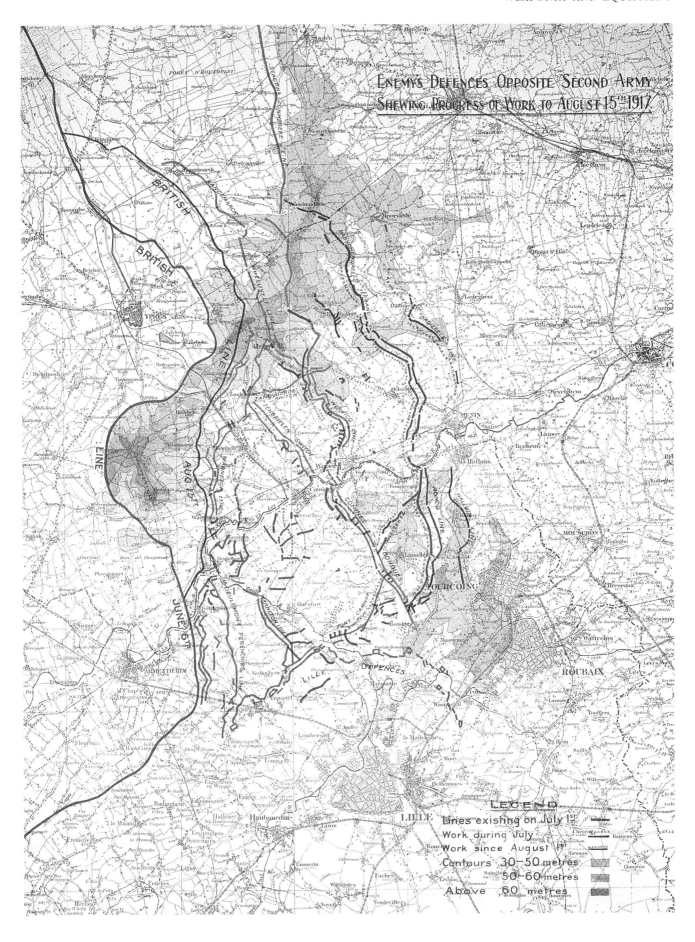

issue. Then one threw a bomb oneself and jumped forward. Scarce a glance fell on the huddled body of the enemy. He was done for, and now a fresh duel began... Then came the climax. The enemy, hard pressed, and with us always on his heels, made ready to retire by a communication trench that turned away to the right. I jumped on to a fire step and saw that this trench for a good stretch ran parallel to ours at a distance of only twenty meters. So the enemy had to pass by us once more.

"We could look right down on the helmets of the English, who stumbled over each other in their haste and excitement. I lobbed a bomb at the feet of the foremost. They started back and crowded on those behind. Now began an indescribable carnage. Bombs flew through the air like snowballs till the whole scene was veiled in white smoke. Two men handed me bombs ready to throw without a moment's pause. Bombs flashed and exploded among the mob of English, throwing them aloft in fragments with their helmets. Cries of rage and terror were mingled. With fire in our eyes, we sprang with a shout over the top. In the midst of this tumult I was struck to the earth by a terrific blow. Sobered, I tore off my helmet, and saw in horror two large holes in it..."

Though the Mills bomb, stick grenade, and the US and French fragmentation grenades became staples of combat which would last long after the trench war was over, it has to be remembered that, like most of the munitions of the period, there were constant attempts at technological advance. In the British case it was thought that the Mills, effective though it undoubtedly was, could be improved upon. Technically it was imagined that anything that had a spring that was kept under tension for long periods must be flawed. Likewise the fact that it had a time fuse was also seen as a potential disadvantage. There were therefore continual efforts to design a new bomb, which did not require a spring loaded striker, and would explode on impact with the ground or target. None of these were a complete success.

A new German bomb which did see widespread use from 1916 was the so-called "egg" grenade—a device, as its name would suggest,

which was the approximate size of a hen's egg. This was no great feat of technology as it still used an old-fashioned friction pull and had a simple time fuse. Nevertheless its size offered distinct advantages, since large numbers could be carried, and its relatively light weight made it possible to throw further than conventional grenades. It soon acquired its own small tactical niche, for long range work, and using over the heads of stick grenade throwers in a bomb duel. That it had some effect may be judged from the fact that not long after its introduction the British were also experimenting with a similar idea, and came up with their own "No. 34" egg bomb.

Yet another facet of the grenade struggle was the "rifle grenade"—a type of explosive projectile which could be fired from a rifle. The earliest versions had a rod on the rear which was inserted into the muzzle of the gun, which was then fired with a blank cartridge shooting the grenade into the enemy lines. There were multiple advantages to the rifle grenade: it went further than a hand grenade; it formed part of a handy man portable system; and had considerable surprise and harassment effects.

On the debit side, such grenades carried only small explosive charges, took some time to perfect, and in some varieties had a propensity to malfunction. The rifle grenade idea had existed prewar, and is credited to British inventor Frederick Marten Hale—hence the expression "Hale grenade"—but few armies showed much interest before 1914. The ironic result was that the Germans produced some bombs based on Hale's ideas, and Allied answers had to be hurriedly produced.

Many new models followed. One of the most imaginative, if alarming, of these was the French "VB" type. This consisted of a small grenade, shaped like a round-topped cylinder, with a hole right through the middle. This was loaded into a bell-mouthed projector cup, or "tromblon," on the rifle muzzle, and the rifle was then fired using a normal bulleted round. The bullet shot out through the center of the bomb, but as it did so it trapped expanding gases behind the base of the bomb throwing it out high into the air. The fuse was simultaneously ignited so that the grenade exploded around the time of arrival. Again, an unlikely idea was influential, since before long the Germans were also using a similar device which the Allies Christened the "Jam Pot" bomb. In this case the British went their own way, adapting the Mills by means of a short rod, or base plate, so that eventually the infantryman really needed only one sort of bomb which could be hand or rifle thrown as the need arose. This had distinct advantages in terms of bulk manufacture and commonality of training.

ARTILLERY

Heinz Guderian, serving on the German Crown Prince's staff at Verdun, was just one of many who chanced on the metaphor that it was artillery which converted the "beautiful countryside into a moonscape," but the cliché deserves greater elaboration. Artillery specialist Herbert Sulzbach filled in more detail:

"For conditions on the Somme it seems to be a quiet day. Nevertheless, our first impression is one of devastation, destruction, and unspeakable horror. Pertain! Whatever does the place look like! The dismembered horses lie higgledy-piggledy all over the road, all equally dead, and what ought to be a village street is nothing but a boggy field full of shell holes; you can hardly walk along it, you keep stumbling. Then it starts humming and quaking. The heaviest caliber stuff is coming over; you do more lying than walking. Our battery is stationed on the outskirts of Pertain, among the ruins and more shell holes than you can count. German batteries of every caliber are standing close as bits of bacon on a larded joint... Up at the front here there isn't a square meter of earth that hasn't been ploughed up: all that's left of the ground surface is shell holes."

With professional detachment Sulzbach noted that his own 63rd Field Artillery regiment was firing an average of a thousand rounds a day. Pertain was getting 3,000 in return.

Below: **Smaller scale map of the trenches of 7 Division, 20th Infantry Brigade. The map covers the period from January to October 1916—and so spans much of the time of the Battle of the Somme.**

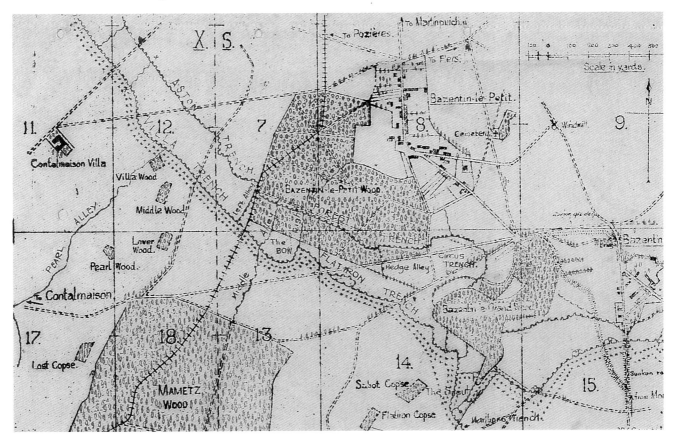

Above: **The real horror—Allied soldiers blasted from their position and looted. Even the boots have been taken as valuable salvage by the enemy.**

On the personal level there was nothing on the battlefield like shelling. As French soldier Marc Richard described the experience:

"Imagine, if you can, a storm, a tempest, growing steadily worse, in which the rain consists entirely of cobblestones, in which the hail is made up entirely of masonry blocks. Remember that a mere 120mm (shell), at the point of impact, has gathered the same energy and releases, just as instantaneously, the same destructive force as an express train hitting the buffers at 90 kilometers an hour... And we're underneath it."

There are probably more descriptions of shell explosions amongst soldiers' memoirs than of any other single subject. An especially evocative word picture of just one detonation was drawn by Guy Chapman:

"There came one shattering clang. In the infinitesimal fraction of a second, I saw the pigeoneer, his hands fluttering, his face like a martyr's in the fire, leap upward to the ceiling, and young Morgan, the runner, pitching forward on top of me. The candles shot up and died. I remember running trembling hands over my belly and legs, automatically searching for a wound. A complete silence fell. Then from the passage came one sigh, the simultaneous passing of life from the dozen wounded men lying there. Another silence, in which the pigeons began to coo and flutter; and at that there broke out from the aid post a high shrilling. One of the orderlies had been half-scythed in two by a piece of shell which had cleft him through the buttocks."

A direct hit, or near miss, from a high explosive shell could not only kill instantly, but mutilate the human body beyond recognition. Paul Dubrulle recorded the impact of a shell as "a terrible jolt," followed by a chaos of smoke, earth, stones, and branches—and all too frequently, limbs, flesh, and a rain of blood. Army Service Corps driver Harry Ainsworth was just one of many veterans to recall shreds of humanity left hanging in trees. Captain Pollard, serving with the Honourable Artillery Company, recorded finding just a head standing upright, in glorious isolation, in the bottom of a shell hole. The image haunted him for a long time afterward: nevertheless, this at least seemed to be a quick death. Gunner George Wear, serving with the Royal Artillery on the Somme, recalled that his Lieutenant was "literally blown to pieces" so that "bits of flesh" besmeared the gun pit. The remains had to be collected in a sandbag. In many similar instances, chaplains would say a few words over such a bundle unsure whether it was one body or several which they were consigning to the ground.

The effect of the shell explosion on the mind and the suddenness of injury could leave a man completely confused as to what had happened to him. Sergeant J. F. Bell of the Gordon Highlanders crossed some ground between the front line trench and a communication trench, when he thought he received a "blow on the head." Feeling that he was "not running properly," he looked down to find his right foot was missing. Not surprisingly the power of speech abandoned him, and he stood rooted to the spot on one leg, watching men run by, until he fainted and fell to the ground. Even for the strong-minded, shelling was an "absolutely helpless" experience. The big shells could completely bury a man, leaving him not knowing whether he was dead, alive, or about to die by smothering. Private Jack Rogers with the Sherwood Foresters recalled a big shell which fell right on the parapet:

"There was a terrific bang, the earth and dirt suddenly collapsed right in on top of Ginotti and myself. We were completely buried. . . other pals

Below: **The effects of remorseless shelling: an aerial photo of Passchendaele, before and after the bombardment.**

... knew just where we were so they apparently hurried along and dug and dug until they came on Ginotti's boot. They knew he must be somewhere close behind so they kept on... I was buried for a long time but luckily I was wearing my steel helmet. This was pushed down in front of my nose by the falling earth, but saved my life because it kept the dirt from going into my face, and gave me a tiny space in which to breathe."

Henry Dundas found that shelling was not "much fun"—and that going into a dugout merely exchanged disintegration for "burial alive."

What is often not so well appreciated is that artillery technology had advanced rapidly in the decades before 1914, and that the war would accelerate this improvement. By 1914, field guns had advanced to the state where they could fire rapidly and reliably to long range, but they were still commonly used over "open sights"—that is directly at targets they could see. After the outbreak of war and particularly after the onset of trench warfare, there were dramatic improvements in "observed" and "predicted" fire. With a separate "Forward Observer," it was possible to direct the guns remotely, usually relaying instructions by means of telephone. With reliable maps and survey equipment it became possible to predict where fire was going to land. So it was that later in the war batteries could be redeployed to new positions in secrecy, and open fire without elaborate preliminaries—thus achieving considerable surprise.

The ability to locate enemy batteries also improved gradually with time and two of the major breakthroughs concerned "sound ranging" and "flash spotting." One of the first to suggest that distant batteries could be located by sound was Austrian musician Fritz Kreisler who noticed that shells made different noises along the path of their flight. On firing the noise of an ascending shell produced a dull whine with a "falling cadence"—coming down the sound was rising, and shrill. Such observation could give some

clues as to whether a gun was near or far. Later, more sophisticated methods, pioneered by the French, would see the use of two or more listening positions which would plot the distances to a firing battery on a map, and locate its position by triangulation. The British similarly set up "sound ranging" sections, which adopted the new Tucker microphones in mid–1916.

By 1918, long-range artillery fire was a complex, scientific business requiring remarkable organization. Serving with a 155mm howitzer battery, US artilleryman Amos Wilder described how the 90lb shells were brought up to the camouflaged guns at night and laid in stores just below ground level, along with separate stores of bagged charges and fuses, to avoid the prying eyes of enemy pilots. Forward observers would be positioned well to the front in an observation post, connected back to the battery by means of wires strung a distance of miles through the woods and fields.

When fire was needed the telephone would ring or a courier would arrive with orders for so many shells, of whatever type, on a certain location, at a specified time. The targets might be trenches, batteries, or communications and assembly points, anything up to seven miles away. Maps were then studied, and atmospheric conditions taken into account so that calculations could be made. Trial rounds would be fired to get the guns right on target, and the forward observers would send back reports on whether the ranging shots were "over" or "short" or otherwise inaccurate. When the guns were aimed satisfactorily, action would start in earnest, with all members of the crews going to their tasks with a will:

"When a gun was fired one member of the crew adjusted the barrel for the required direction and trajectory; another rammed home the shell after screwing on its fuse; another added the powder charge (a bag not actually of powder but of thin yellow strips); a fourth closed the breech block; then all seven of the crew put their fingers in their ears as the last, at the officer's command, pulled the lanyard. All had cotton in their ears..."

Of equal importance to the actual firing was the "fire plan"—the score to which the

---

Left: **A Royal Engineer drawing a plan using a plane table. Improved surveying was the basis of both accurate trench maps and enabled artillery to engage in "predicted fire."**

Above: **Australian 8-inch howitzers of the 54th Siege Battery during the Third Battle of Ypres, 1917.**

Right: **Captured howitzer at Flesquieres. Note the pit and attempt at camouflage.**

cacophony of destruction would be played. By synchronizing the fire of hundreds of guns in many batteries it proved possible to produce many new and remarkable effects. By 1916, creeping barrages (slowly advancing curtains of shells behind which troops could advance) had made their appearance. With "box" barrages sectors of the line could be cut off from support, allowing designated areas to be assaulted or raided without interference from others. Wire cutting with artillery fire, used somewhat falteringly in 1916, became a really practical proposition later on. With better shells, special fuses for designated tasks, bigger concentrations of heavier shells, and—perhaps above all—decent coordination with the infantry, the artillery became a key weapon in helping to reopen the fronts which had been locked for so long.

Another form of artillery which will forever be associated with 1914–1918 is the trench mortar, though prewar experiments had taken place, and the Germans certainly possessed examples prior to the outbreak of war. The essence of the trench mortar was that it was a weapon which could be fired at high trajectory, to land its projectiles in the enemy lines, hitting targets which would be well nigh inaccessible to any other type of weapon. Trench mortar crews were viewed with a distinct ambivalence by their infantry colleagues, for while they could inflict damage they were also likely to be the occasion for enemy retaliation. Very often the mortars themselves would not hang around to see what this retaliation was like.

Nevertheless, trench mortars and particularly the heavier types, could be impressive instruments of destruction. An early German example was watched with due astonishment by Karl Josenhans:

Below: **German photograph showing a captured battlefield dump of finned projectiles for the 57mm French trench mortar.**

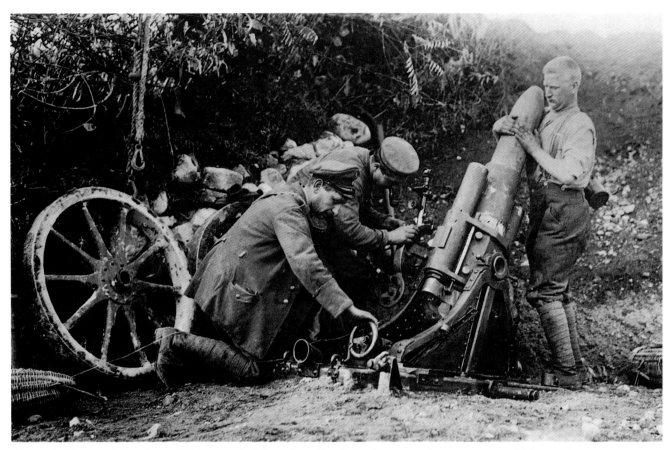

Above: **A German 25cm heavy "Minenwerfer" in action. On difficult sectors the mortars would be carried up in parts.**

"One murderous instrument with which we have the advantage is the big trench mortar. They hurl huge shells about a thousand feet into the air and they fall almost vertically... Earth and branches are flung into the air to the height of a house, and although the shells fell eighty yards away from us, the ground under us shook. During the explosions, I was looking through a periscope into the French trench opposite and could see the terrified men running away to the rear. But somebody was evidently standing behind them with a revolver, for one after another they came crawling back again. This war is simply a matter of hounding men to death, and that is a degrading business."

For Captain Billie Nevill of the East Surreys, writing in October 1915, trench mortars were "inventions of the devil:"

"They chuck a variety of eggs, varying from a thing about the size of a 3lb jam pot to an aerial torpedo, which has 250lb of explosive alone in it! The advantage about them is that you can see

them in the air... everyone calls a trench mortar's egg a sausage... they make the most colossal noise and the concussion is enormous. Pearce, for instance, was blown down some steps into a dugout, Bertie Clare was chucked through the door of his..."

Yet as with so many other things, the trench mortar underwent considerable change over time. In the British instance some of the first models were made of such unpromising raw materials as drain pipes, and were primarily notable for their failure. By the middle of the war better types had evolved. These included the outlandish, but highly destructive, two-inch model, better known as the "Toffee Apple" or "Plum Pudding" bomb thrower. As the name suggests the projectile for this weapon resembled a huge toffee apple. Though the steel "stick" was only about two inches in diameter, the head was the size of a football, weighed 50lb, and was packed with explosive. This bomb was reasonably regarded as the maximum which could conveniently be handled by

Left: Two of the main models of German trench mortar in the latter part of the war: on the left the medium 17cm and on the right the heavy 25cm models. These weapons belonged to Minenwerfer Company 244, which served with the 44th Reserve Division facing both the British and French from 1917-1918.

Below: A Paul Hoffman postcard showing the Kaiser inspecting captured British heavy trench mortars. In addition to the French-designed 9.45 inch mortars, Lewis guns can be seen resting against a tree.

Zensiert
aul Hoffmann & Co.
Berlin-Schöneberg.

Above: **Troops carrying the component parts for the Stokes trench mortar. It had a range of about 800 yards.**

one man in the confines of a trench. The stick was placed into the stubby barrel of the mortar, while the head overhung the outside of the tube. To fire the mortar a pull was given to a lanyard attached to a rifle type firing mechanism which set off the propulsive charge. The toffee apple now shot off at high angle into the enemy lines—with a direct hit more than capable of collapsing trench dugouts, or blowing out sections of sandbags.

Arguably the real breakthrough was the Stokes mortar. This was a dramatic improvement on what had gone before, with an impressive performance, as was reported by Seaforth's officer Norman Collins on a course in June 1918:

> "Each gun has a crew of five. No. 1 gives the orders, No. 2 sights and fires the gun, No. 3 helps to fix it up and 4 and 5 fix up the shells for firing. I am No. 2. The shells are quite big affairs over a foot long and weigh about 12lb. The range is 800 yards. The fire is so rapid that one gun can get eight shells in the air at once before the first one hits the ground. I drop the shells in the muzzle and they slide down… and hit a striker at the bottom which explodes the propelling cartridge at the bottom of the shell which flies out. About six shells will blow a house to bits."

So it was that the Stokes mortar combined power with rate of fire, and reasonable portability. It could be used from a pit, carried up behind attacking troops, and brought into action quickly. There is little wonder that after 1918 that it came to be regarded as the model for most mortars.

GAS

Gas, now familiar as a weapon of terror, was a new idea in the Great War. So new in fact that there was dispute as to whether such a thing was actually against the then existing laws of war. Conventions banned the use of "projectiles" whose main purpose was the dissemination of poisons—but whether poison gas itself was a "projectile," and whether a projectile which had other possible purposes was allowed was not clear. Though several nations made experiments, the potential loophole was most systematically exploited by Germany, which made the first large-scale release of chlorine gas from cylinders on the Western Front in April 1915. For those on the receiving end, the rolling, billowing cloud of greenish yellow was a hideous experience. Chlorine attacked the respiratory system and eyes, leaving the victims choking. The French Colonials in the path of the first attack were totally unprotected and broke and fled. The line was held further back, at some expense, only by the intervention of the Canadians.

The sense of helplessness against the first gas attacks was little diminished by the first British instructions issued on gas defense on April 26, 1915, pending the issue of "special appliances:"

1. Immediately the presence of asphyxiating gas is suspected, if no better means of protection is available, take a pocket handkerchief or other small piece of cloth, roll it into a ball, and hold it in the mouth, drawing breath in and out through it until it is quite moist. As soon as the cloth is moist, draw the breath in through it, breathing in through the mouth and out through the nose, so that all the air drawn in has to pass through the damp cloth. This has the effect of removing the harmful gas from the entering air. Soldiers liable to be exposed to asphyxiating gases should practice breathing in through a piece of cloth and breathing out through the nose as this is difficult at first, but with practice becomes easy.

2. For prolonged exposure to asphyxiating gas, in place of the handkerchief, use a piece of flannel about one yard square, folded in such a way as to pass over the mouth from ear to ear under the nose, and tie at the back of the head. Moisten by

Below: **Men of the 55th West Lancashire Division, suffering from the effects of gas, 1918.**

breathing in and out through it for a few moments, or, if time allows, by pouring a few spoonfuls of water into the inner folds, and then breath in through the mouth and out through the nose as above..."

Another, and even more bizarre, trick recommended in early May was to knock the bottom off a beer bottle and put into it a pad of cotton wool, then some earth, and then more cotton wool. This was held in the mouth for breathing.

Despite outrage over the German use of gas, retaliation in kind was seen as inevitable. As Lieutenant General Fergusson commander of II Corps put it:

"It is a cowardly form of warfare which does not commend itself to me or other English soldiers... but... We cannot win this war unless we kill or incapacitate more of our enemies than they do of us, and if this can only be done by our copying the enemy in his choice of weapons, we must not refuse to do so."

So it was that Britain formed her "Special Companies" of Royal Engineer gas troops and also set about developing her own offensive gas capability. By the autumn, gas was also wafting west to east across the front. In British use chlorine would be codenamed "Red Star."

It would be entirely wrong to assume that once both sides were using chlorine, the gas war assumed stasis. Constant research was aimed at discovering both new and more deadly gases, and more efficient ways to deliver them. Experiments with phosgene were soon underway, and its greater toxicity was soon apparent, as was its relative difficulty in detection. Its down side was that it was light, and thus had a tendency to dissipate harmlessly before reaching the enemy.

Left: Argyll and Sutherland Highlanders with some of the first gas masks issued to British troops. The later introduction of mustard gas made it difficult for the Scottish regiments to go into battle wearing kilts.

The answer was to mix phosgene with the heavier chlorine to create a more lethal and persistent cloud. Phosgene was in use by the Germans from the end of 1915, and from 1916, it was also in general use as a cylinder-released gas.

First identified as "HS" or "Hun Stuff," mustard gas made its unwelcome debut in German hands in July 1917. This substance represented a step change in gas warfare, as it did not merely attack the respiratory system and eyes, but was a "blister agent" which damaged the skin anywhere it touched. The result was burns and blisters which could put a man out of action very easily. One unit unfortunate enough to get an early taste of the "garlic smelling" mustard was the Liverpool Scottish who suffered about 70 casualties from a gas bombardment on July 21. As the regimental history put it:

"It was impossible to avoid casualties in a heavy concentration of this gas. The box respirator protected the throat and eyes but the dense fumes which hung about in the trenches and shell holes attacked the skin—especially the softer parts of it — and caused painful sores. In these circumstances the kilt is not an ideal garment."

Despite the horrors and numerous casualties wrought by gas, it was no war-winning wonder weapon. Cylinder discharges were difficult and time-consuming to arrange, and suffered from the vagaries of the weather. Men who were not killed outright and donned their gas masks, or made it to medical aid, had a very good chance of survival. Familiarity brought not contempt but a very wary alertness. This was doubtless one of the spurs to another race to find the optimum method of delivery. As early as 1915, gas shells fired from artillery appeared to offer a solution. Unlike cylinder clouds, gas shells landed on the opposition lines before releasing their deadly cargo. Moreover they arrived suddenly and with relatively little warning. H.S. Clapham recorded:

"The Huns started to bombard us with a shell which was quite new to us. It sounded like a gigantic fire cracker, with two distinct explosions. These shells came over just above the parapet... after a

121

Above: **French 75mm field gun, dating from 1897, firing on the Oise front. The gunners wear the "ARS" type mask issued in the latter part of the war.**

quarter of an hour of this sort of thing, there was a sudden crash in the trench and ten feet of the parapet, just beyond me, was blown away and everyone around blinded by the dust. With my first glance I saw what looked like half a dozen bodies, mingled with sand bags, and then I smelt gas and realized these were gas shells... One man was sick all over the sand bags and another coughed his heart up. We pulled four men out of the debris unharmed. One man was unconscious and died of gas later."

Other commentators have noted that gas shells were in fact quieter than the high explosive variety, and if exploded at any distance from the hearer sounded more like a "pop" than the usual, deafening crash and roar. It became normal practice to mix gas shell bombardments with both smoke and explosives, thus creating more surprise and uncertainty. Orders would be issued to don masks, then it would be discovered that the suspected gas was harmless smoke—to confuse and shield the movement of troops. At times men

would be tempted to remove their masks, only to discover the explosives were mixed with gas.

Where gas shells were inadequate was in terms of the concentrations of gas, they could generate. Compared to cylinders individual gas shells were small, and many were required to build up significant areas of lethal concentration. What was really needed was a device which would achieve both hefty concentrations on the enemy lines and surprise. The answer was the "gas projector," a tube, like a very wide-mouthed mortar which could fire out a cylinder. The British "Livens" version was deployed in batteries, sunk into the ground, and fired electrically at the vital moment. The effects of large amounts of gas arriving at a distance can be imagined, and it is not surprising that other nations later emulated the Livens.

Like gas itself, gas masks improved steadily with time but it was often a painful process. The second generation British gas or smoke "helmets" of later 1915 and 1916 pulled on right over the head, giving far better protection, but they also had significant drawbacks. These impregnated flannel bags were not proof against gas indefinitely, and they were sticky, hot, and unpleasant. As Harry Cooper with the South Africans would relate:

> "While taking it easy I noticed a peculiar smell not unlike pineapples and my eyes started to water. Someone yelled, "Gas" and did the old "PH" gas helmets come out from the satchels we carried! . . . They were in the form of a sack with goggles. They had to be taken from the satchels, placed over the head and the base tucked into the tunic. Speed in doing this counted for everything. And this time the regulation was beaten hands down. After a while I noticed the men removing the smelly old masks and I tried to get mine off but the damned thing had stuck to my eyebrows."

Vaseline was said to help keep the bag from sticking, but of course there was seldom opportunity for such niceties. In any event, the appearance of the soldier in the gas helmet was nightmarish. As Captain Donaldson of the Warwickshires observed, you looked like "some horrible kind of demon or goblin." Some photographs show men wearing the gas helmet on the head, rolled up when gas is not actually in the air. In such a position "tube" helmets with their projecting exhalation valve took on an appearance not unlike the bill of a duck. Anthony Eden remembered the inconveniences of wearing his on a working party:

> "The worst assignment that summer was to carry gas cylinders up communication trenches and to install them in our front line. This took many weary and exhausting hours. The most disagreeable part of the business was that we had to wear the masks rolled up on the top of our heads under our tin hats all the time. These masks, effective only against chlorine, were damp and impregnated with some unpleasant smelling stuff which, as we were soon to

Below: **A battery of tubes has been sunk into the ground angled towards the enemy. Gas projectiles are being loaded.**

Above: **German artillery. Men and horses in gas masks.**

Right: **Australian chaplain in a gas mask. This mask is the "Harrison's Tower" or "Large Box Respirator." The picture was taken in June 1916.**

124

learn, could bring out an ugly and itching rash on the forehead. The masks had to be at the ready in this way for fear that a chance shell or even machine-gun fire might puncture a cylinder."

The final generation of British masks were the "box" types, and with the box masks a very reliable and durable system of personal defense was eventually found. The first of the series was the "Large Box" or "Harrison's Tower," which consisted of a steel filter box carried in a bag slung around the neck, a tube, and a close fitting face mask. The secret of the filter box was the granules, which it contained, that absorbed toxic substances, before air was taken up the tube and into the lungs. The big advantage was that the filter box could be large, and that since it was carried in a separate bag the soldier did not have a dead weight hanging from his face. "Harrison's Tower" was issued mainly to the artillery, but the improved "Small Box Respirator" or "SBR," which followed was given to all troops.

So effective was the SBR that it was also used by the US army. Another significant property of the SBR was its adaptability since it was possible to up-rate it against new gases by fitting a new box, or to add further types of filter to the existing arrangement. How highly the box respirator was valued by the ordinary soldier became apparent during the German Spring offensive of 1918. Officers attempting to rally British troops who were falling back were interested to discover that a good many had retained their rifles—but many more had kept their gas masks. Indeed almost none had fled without their SBR.

OTHER TRENCH EQUIPMENT

New types of artillery, machine guns, mortars, and gas remained as lasting legacies of the trench war. Another weapon which appeared very late was the submachine gun, a small, hand-held machine weapon which could be carried within the trench by one man. Luckily for the Allies, the Germans had no chance to fully exploit this before the war ended and it was not until

Left: **French soldier with periscope rifle. Also known as a "hyposcope," this device enabled shots to be taken from below the level of the parapet.**

125

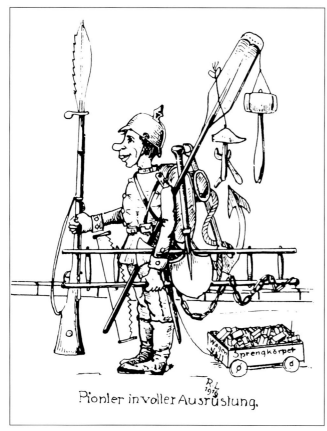

Above: **"The pioneer in full equipment"**—a German cartoon of 1916, showing a pioneer laden with various objects, including rifle with saw bayonet, ladder, and towing a cart of explosives.

World War II before it would see its full potential.

There were also many strange beasts, which would either sink into obscurity, or see relatively limited application after 1918. Some of the more unusual and inventive pieces of equipment included the "hyposcope" rifle, a device fired from below the level of the trench using a periscope; the "rifle battery" which could be set up with one or more rifles and then fired later as required onto preset targets; and the trench sweeping shotgun, ideal for clearing confined spaces of all human life.

Another weapon, now believed totally extinct, was the catapult or "bomb engine." Bomb engines were effectively a miniature form of mechanically powered artillery, throwing grenades or other explosive devices without the aid of explosive propellants. Many took their inspiration from the siege engines of old, and theoretically they had much to recommend them, being able to fling missiles into the enemy lines in virtual silence. The practical experience was different—twanging elastics and springs, long arms and explosives were often difficult or downright dangerous to handle in the trench environment. Moreover, the result when achieved was often disappointing and not in scale to the effort deployed. Few catapults handled a projectile of much more than 2lb weight and 200 yards was a fair range. Against this had to be set rifle grenades which achieved a similar performance with far less bulky equipment, and trench mortars which had far better ranges and destructive power. Bomb engines, which had a brief heyday in late 1914 and 1915, sank into obscurity during 1916.

One device which saw widespread use was the Bangalore Torpedo. This was effectively an elongated charge, which could be pushed through an obstacle, such as a barbed wire entanglement, then detonated to forge a path. One German version was fabricated using the heads of stick grenades attached to a plank. Though Bangalores were sometimes effective, the users of such dangerous devices could take a dim view of the boffin's inventiveness as Frank Richards related:

"We were in the Cambrin trenches and a Bangalore Torpedo was sent up to the Battalion, which had to be taken out and attached to the German barbed wire. This torpedo had been tried and proved a great success in some back area or other where there were no shells or bullets flying about and also no enemy waiting to ram a foot of steel through a man's chest. It was claimed that this torpedo could destroy more wire than a battery of artillery would, firing for a week. Our comments were that if the inventor and the men who had tried it out in the back areas had the job of hitching it on the enemy's wire here at Cambrin they'd not reach half way across no man's land before they'd be returning to change their underpants."

In the event, the Royal Welch Fusiliers did manage to deliver this particular Bangalore to its destination. However, they eventually got it back again, some alert Germans having defused it in the mean time.

Some whole classes of trench warfare equipment disappeared without trace almost as soon as they were invented. Among these were counted

Above: **Major Bishop, a Canadian, was the highest scoring ace to fly with the RFC. He was awarded the Victoria Cross.**

large fans supposed to disperse gas; hand grenades whose fuses were lit by an electric charge from a battery; centrifugal throwers which relied on spinning wheels; and bayonets which could be fitted to pistols. Such were the many monuments to destructive ingenuity.

AIRCRAFT

The advent of air warfare was one of the most dramatic changes to conflict for many years. Nevertheless, World War I was not the first instance of the use of military aircraft. On a small scale, bomb, and leaflet dropping, and the taking of aerial reconnaissance photographs had all occurred in 1911, in the Italo-Turkish war. In the major powers, the air forces grew out of pre-existing military balloon services. The British Royal Flying Corps, which had started from the Balloon Section of the Royal Engineers, was formed in 1912. German army aviation commenced with balloon evaluation as early as 1884. Following experiments with airships the German

army air service acquired its first aircraft in 1910. The French *Corps d'Aérostation*, which operated balloons, first achieved an independent identity in 1910 and within the next few years a relatively advanced aviation service, or *Aviation Militaire*, sprung into existence.

By the outbreak of war, there were small but significant numbers of aircraft in service over European skies. The British had about 60 machines. These were a mixture of British models such as the BE2 and Avro 504, and French types like the Blériot XI monoplane and the Henri Farman F20. Many of the British craft were conventional biplanes, but the Henri Farman was a "pusher" with its propeller to the rear, and relatively under-powered. The French air service had the better part of 200 aircraft, most of which were organized into escadrilles or squadrons of six machines. Soon after the start of the war these included Breguet and Farman biplanes and the Bleriot, Nieuport, Deperdussin, and Hanriot monoplanes. The enthusiastic amateurism of the early British pilots was underlined

Far Left: **Aerial camera on BE2c. The flier operates the "C" type camera from the open cockpit.**

Left: **Air photo examination. Air warfare began with attempts to observe the enemy.**

Below: **Trench map of Montauban and the Somme area, June, 1916.**

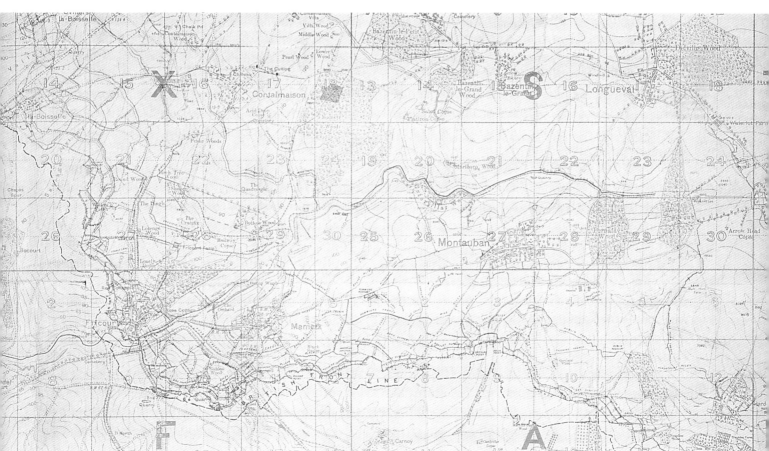

Above: **An FE2d of number 20 squadron. The observer was obliged to stand in order to use the Lewis gun.**

by the fact that they had learned to fly with civilian clubs before joining the RFC. The Corps road transport was a mixture of requisitioned vehicles, and included a very conspicuous HP Sauce van. The German strength was much greater with 230 planes, its "field flights" again organized into six-strong units, though not all these were deployed in the west, given the existence of a Russian air service equipped mainly with French-designed machines.

In August 1914, virtually all military air activity was aimed at reconnaissance. Like the balloonists that preceded them, the aircraft aviators were primarily intended to get into the air near enemy troop formations, and report their position and progress to headquarters. What had received little attention before the war was the idea that air observers would themselves become targets, and would naturally attempt to defend themselves. There were a few voices in the wilderness, like that of Captain Bertram Dickson, who believed that:

"In the event of European war, both sides would be equipped with large corps of airplanes, each trying to obtain information from the other and hide its own movements. The efforts which each would exert would lead to the inevitable result of war in the air, for the supremacy of the air, by armed airplanes against each other."

Dickson was correct, but his prescience led to no general arming of military aircraft. The result was some early tragicomic combats in which pilots and aircrews took aloft shotguns, pistols, and even grenades, and tried, usually unsuccessfully, to hit other pilots or targets on the ground. In the first months of the war, it was the two-seaters which had the advantage, since the second man could handle a gun while the pilot controlled the plane. In one celebrated incident, an RFC plane crewed by Captain H. C. Jackson and Lieutenant W. R. Read intercepted a German flier and emptied all their rifle and revolver ammunition in the general direction of the enemy. There was no effect, so they flew close and Jackson flung the empty revolver at the German's propeller—again without effect.

Despite the problems some planes were brought down. The British had a peculiar success as early as August 25, 1914, when three BE2s mobbed and forced down a Taube monoplane. The crew ran off and two of the British aviators set light to the enemy machine on the ground. The first air combat victory through shooting was claimed on October 5, 1914, when a French Voisin piloted by Sergeant Joseph Frantz brought down a German Aviatik near Rheims. A war in the air, high over the despised trenches, waged by men usually without parachutes, flying the latest in technology, could not but help to attract a reputation as being the last refuge of chivalry. It was, much of the time, what one RFC officer called "a gentleman's job," especially early on, when it was considered unsporting to continue to fire on damaged aircraft which broke off combat. Moreover, messages were sometimes dropped over opposition airfields with news of the fate of aircrews.

Even British infantry officers could empathize with the courage of the enemy. Looking up from the ground, Captain Nevill found that he could not "work up any animosity against the hun airplanes, they are great sportsmen." Zeppelins which bombed civilian targets were a different matter, "though that must require a lot of nerve." For Private Raymond Grimshaw, watching from trenches in 1915, the "nerve" needed for air combat was made horribly apparent during a dog fight:

> "Ascending to about 3,000 feet, the Briton became hidden by cloud. Here he outwitted the German by remaining almost stationary until the Taube passed along underneath him. He then flew down as though he would crash on top of his opponent, but when quite close above him he dropped a bomb. The effect was awful. The Taube burst into flames and dived downward. We expected to see it crash

Below: **French soldiers inspect a crashed Allied biplane.**

Above: **Aviatik Training School, Habsheim, 1915.**

to the ground but with wonderful skill the German got control of his machine—although it was blazing furiously... He got within 1,000 feet of the ground, when he suddenly seemed to fall or jump out of the machine. He dropped like a stone, and the airplane—now out of control—dived straight down, turning over and over in a mass of flames. Though he was German, we admired the gallant attempt he made to get back."

One result of such appreciation of skill and courage was that there were seldom shortages of volunteers for air crew training, though the life expectancy of a pilot was even shorter than that of an officer on the ground. Despite the willingness of many to come forward for the hazardous work, pilots were not plentiful since they took time and aircraft to train. Moreover, men and machines removed from the front to undertake training were badly missed.

One factor more than any other hampered the technical development of successful combat aircraft—if guns were aimed forward from a conventionally designed craft they shot through the arc of the air screw. Incidents in which aviators effectively shot themselves down by shooting off their propeller were not unknown. One solution was the "pusher," with the propeller and pilot to the rear. Another was a device to enable the bullets to pass through the vulnerable propeller without damage. German experiments prior to

the war had led to the development of a prototype synchronizing mechanism as early as 1913, but a simpler solution was devised by the Frenchman Raymond Saulnier. By fitting angled armor to the vulnerable portion of the propeller, it proved possible to deflect bullets away, and thus fire through the obstruction with at least a majority of the rounds.

A real breakthrough was achieved by the Germans following the capture of an aircraft fitted with the Saulnier device in April 1915. Fokker technicians succeeded not only in replicating the Saulnier method, but improved significantly upon it. In the new Fokker, interrupter gear studs on the propeller shaft activated a cam and push rod system. When the push rod was activated, it prevented the machine gun hammer from falling, and thus no shot could be fired when the propeller was in the way. When fitted to the Fokker Eindecker, or monoplane, the result was a highly practical fighting machine. British pilots, flying less battle-worthy machines, came to refer to themselves as "Fokker fodder." Nevertheless any jubilation on the part of the German air service was premature—there were never enough Eindeckers and they were tricky to fly. Important lessons had been learned however, and now victory would often go to the plane

Right: The French-built Morane-Saulnier monoplane, with bullet deflectors built into the propeller.

which had forward firing machine guns. New scouts or "fighters" would be predominantly single-seaters, with the maximum machine-gun power, and the best maneuverability and speed.

Like so many aspects of the trench war, the fight in the air would become very much a matter of technology, production, and industry. A vital area was the continuous improvement in aircraft specification year on year; and this is particularly apparent if one looks at the products of one manufacturer over time.

In the case of Sopwith, the "SS" model of 1914 was pretty typical of the period: it had an 80hp engine, a top speed of 92 mph, and carried no fixed armament. The "One and a Half strutter" two-seater, arguably Sopwith's first, true fighter was produced at the end of 1915. Its 110hp engine gave a top speed of 96 mph, better all-round performance, and it carried a synchronized forward firing fixed machine gun, and a Lewis gun and had a bomb load capacity of 300 lb. The Sopwith Pup, which served in France from mid 1916, had either an 80 or 100hp engine, but boasted a top speed of 104 mph, and sometimes two machine guns. The legendary Sopwith Camel only appeared late in 1916 but would have an unsurpassed combat record, destroying more enemy machines than any other Allied fighting scout. The F1 model featured various engines up to 150hp, and a maximum speed up to 111 mph. The service ceiling was a then-significant 20,000 feet, while it was armed with two machine guns and 80lb of bombs. As specifications and efficiency improved, price remained pretty static, the cost of the One and a Half and the Camel being roughly the same.

As better craft were developed, new tactics were honed in the heat of battle. In the forefront of progress was Oswald Boelke, who pioneered the technique of gaining height, then diving out of the clouds or the sun on a vulnerable angle to dispatch the enemy with short close range bursts.

Right: **Air combat ace Oberleutnant Max Immelmann, the "Eagle of Lille," credited with the invention of the "Immelmann turn"—a climb and half-roll which gained altitude while turning. Seen here wearing the "Blue Max" and both grades of Iron Cross. He was killed in 1916.**

Boelke was also one of the first to fly with a wing man, who would keep his eyes out for danger while his leader attacked. Aggressive pilots learned to attack from the tail of their adversary. An added refinement when taking on two-seaters was to come in from below and behind. If the enemy spotted the attack and rolled to the side to bring the observer's gun to bear the attacker would turn in the opposite direction. The attacker would then turn once more and come in again from below.

Ground attack, which would have a direct impact on the trench war, was much refined from 1917. During the Third Ypres, RFC squadrons were tasked with low level bombing and strafing, both of the front line and supply routes. Many of the attacks were made at under 300 feet and thus commensurately risky to ground fire. German two-seaters such as the Halberstadt were employed on similar duties.

Bombing improved significantly over time, and odd hand grenades and steel darts gradually gave way to larger bombs such as the 25lb and 100lb types. Remarkably some 25lb bombs initially had to be manhandled physically over the side of craft by the crew before the provision of dedicated bomb racks. It was a bombing raid that led to the first RFC Victoria Cross of the war. On April 26, 1915, Lieutenant W.B. Rhodes-Moorhouse bombed the rail junction at Coutrai, but came under machine gun and small arms fire as he swept low over the church. His machine was damaged and he was shot through the thigh. Nevertheless he managed to turn for home, being twice more wounded by ground fire before making it back to British lines. Though mortally wounded he refused medical treatment until he had made a report on his mission.

Another important trend was the move toward larger combat units. The French began concentrating squadrons early in 1916, and in August the Germans formed special purpose

Below: **Pilot and observer of the 69th Australian Squadron ready to start on a night bombing flight. Savy, October 22, 1917.**

Left: **A Sopwith "Camel" biplane looping the loop. A similar plane proved to be the downfall of von Richtofen, who broke his own rules and chased it beyond enemy lines.**

Jagdstaffeln or fighting sections. The following year saw the formation of even bigger fighter wings or Jagdgeschwader. The first of these was under the command of Manfred Freiherr von Richtofen, an aristocratic, top-scoring ace, who was known to fly a red Fokker triplane—hence his Allied nickname "the Red Baron." The whole purpose of the Jagdgeschwader was to win air superiority in a designated sector, and the whole outfit would be moved from place to place. This meant that the Allies would see a mass of planes arrive virtually simultaneously: a veritable "Flying Circus." Part of the German strategy when out-numbered, which was frequently, was to hang back over their own lines. This, as Richtofen famously put it, let the customer "come to the shop." The beneficial result was that when German fliers were forced down, it was usually over their own territory, with surviving crew res-cued and some aircraft salvaged. Conversely Allied craft and pilots were more easily captured.

Von Richtofen went on to become arguably the best-known flier of the war—and probably the most famous ace in the history of air warfare. Between September 1915 and April 1918 his personal tally reached approximately 83 Allied aircraft, with 80 officially confirmed "kills." The highest decoration, the coveted *Pour Le Mérite*, or "Blue Max," was awarded to him on January 18, 1918. He used several different personalized planes, and the majority of his victims were British. His finest hour was April 29, 1917, when he shot down four RFC aircraft from different squadrons on the same day. That July he was himself shot down during a major dogfight, by a long-range burst from the machine of Captain D. C. Cunnell and Lieutenant A. E. Woodbridge, as his letters record:

> "Suddenly, something strikes me in the head. For a moment my whole body is paralyzed. My arms hang down limply beside me; my legs flop loosely

Right: **Rittmeister Manfred Freiherr von Richtofen. The most successful air ace of World War I.**

beyond my control. The worst was that a nerve leading to my eyes had been paralyzed and I was completely blind. I feel my machine tumbling down—falling. At that moment, the idea struck me, this is how it feels when one is shot down to his death. At any moment I wait for my wings to break off."

This time, however, he survived. Drifting in and out of consciousness he was able to regain control long enough to clear the shell holes, tear through some telephone wires, and be rescued from the wreck.

On April 21, 1918, his luck finally ran out. Chasing a Sopwith Camel too boldly down to the ground, he was himself set upon by Captain A. R. Brown, and then fired on by Australian troops from the ground. His triplane side-slipped, hit the earth in a beet field beside the Bray-Corbie road, bounced, broke its undercarriage, and finally crashed, slewing round as it did so. A bullet had pierced his side through to the spine, and been deflected forward out of his chest. Other multiple injuries had been caused by the crash—both the Australians and Captain Brown claimed the victory.

THE TANK

Unlike the aircraft, the tank was invented specifically to "solve" the problem of trench warfare. At times there were high expectations that it could do just this, creating a breakthrough so significant that open, mobile warfare would resume. Though this would only happen when many other factors were in place, the tank remains a significant legacy of the war. Despite the fact that the tank was a new invention, pretty much all of its constituent parts had existed prior to 1914. Engine-powered, tracked vehicles were used in logging in the United States; steel armor had been widely used in ships and forts; and breech loading artillery pieces had been the norm for some years. In 1912, a proposal for a tracked vehicle had been put to the War Office, but not acted upon, and in 1914

Left: **British tanks at Meaulte.**

Major E. D. Swinton had given consideration to a vehicle that he called a "machine gun destroyer." What was genuinely remarkable about the events of 1915 and early 1916 was how the disparate elements were finally brought together into a practical new weapon.

Winston Churchill had embraced the idea of "caterpillars" for cutting enemy wire and the domination of the firing line as early as December 1915, but there were several false starts and obstacles to overcome before a fighting machine could be produced. A significant problem was that if the vehicle simply rode upon a pair of tracks, it would be unstable and its obstacle crossing ability severely limited. So it was that although an armored box on tracks, later known as "Little Willie," was running in tests before the end of 1915, it was not found suitable for large scale manufacture. The solution to the problem is generally credited to Lieutenant Walter Wilson, who came up with a large, rhomboid shape around which the tracks were run to create the greatest possible crossing and climbing capacity. In this new layout, the main armament moved to wedge-shaped casements on the sides of the vehicle known as "sponsons." The first of this new type was christened "Mother." The name "tank" was a cover in the hope that the Germans would take these massive, metal boxes to be water tanks.

Colonel Crompton of the Landships Committee nicknamed the new beast the "slug," and in terms of performance he was not far wrong. The production Model Mark I weighed 28 tons and to get the tank to the battlefield at all was a major operation, since its width precluded loading the monster straight onto a railway wagon. The solution was to unbolt the side sponsons, load the tank without them, and refit them on arrival. Once at the front the Mark I had a top speed of under four miles per hour on good ground, and used just over two gallons of petrol per mile covered. "Male" tanks were armed with two 6 pounder guns and four machine guns, "female" types had five machine guns only. The crew was eight men. The armor had a maximum thickness of 10mm, enough to stop small arms and splinters but nothing to impede a direct hit from an artillery shell or mortar. Moreover, the armor was riveted to unarmored angle irons, and compromised by the fact that vision was direct through small flaps. Bullets striking the plates near a hole could create a dangerous "splash" of molten metal. This was a major reason why tank crews were later issued with face masks comprising metal goggles with slits and a hanging chain defense for the lower face.

Whether to use the new weapon as soon as possible, before surprise could be lost, or whether to wait until tanks were available in overwhelming numbers, presented the High Command with a terrible dilemma. In the end, it was decided that 49 tanks would make the debut at Flers on the Somme, on September 15, 1916. These were to be used in twos and threes against strong points, but in the event just 32 made it to the start line. One of these was "Dracula" commanded by

Lieutenant A. E. Arnold—who took nine hours to travel from Green Dump to his jumping-off point beyond Delville Wood only three miles away. By the time Dracula arrived the infantry were already out of their trenches:

"We were into the German counter barrage … As we crossed no man's land the other tank of my pair was just in front and a little way to the right and getting along well now that the ground was better. Suddenly she stopped and was emitting clouds of smoke. I saw the crew—or some of them—tumble out of the back door. This was not encouraging… The German front line trenches had been shelled practically out of existence and I think the infantry met little opposition there. And Dracula reached the support line first. A row of German heads appeared above the parapet and

---

Below: **British tank stuck in a trench, November 1917. The troops are from 1st Battalion, the Leicestershire Regiment.**

looked—no doubt in amazement— at what was approaching out of the murk of the bombardment. At point blank range I drew a bead with my Hotchkiss and pressed the trigger. It did not fire!… I dismounted the gun and discovered the trouble. A shell splinter had struck the exposed portion and dented the metal guard over the piston. I mounted the spare gun."

Dracula now pressed on to Flers and sheltered behind a belt of trees. Shortly afterward there was news of a German counterattack, and Arnold's tank was back in action:

"We emerged from our lair, crossed the sunken road, and went out to the front. We were rewarded with the sight of long lines of Germans advancing in open formation and opened fire with our port side Vickers guns at 900 yards range. It was impossible to tell just what effect our fire took but it certainly checked the advance. Dracula cruised about for a while in front of the village and then came under what seemed to me to be direct fire from a field gun. A difficult matter to judge, but someone was making useful practice against us. One shell in particular seemed to miss us by inches. I had, in the meantime, collected a bullet through my knee while outside. It was now late afternoon and as our infantry had been reinforced I judged it was time to get back."

The tank had proved a success. Many German infantry had broken and run at the sight of these weird monsters, but the overall result of the first attack has been realistically assessed as a "local success" rather than an overwhelming victory.

Below: **British Mark I tank with the original steering tail, September 25, 1916.**

Above: **A British "Wire Cutter" tank on the Western Front, being used as an observation platform.**

Nor was the loss one-sided, many tanks broke down through mechanical failure, and five were ditched in the mud. Ten were damaged by enemy action and temporarily put out of action. Neither were fear and discomfort a monopoly of those under attack. An impression of what it was like to go into action in a tank was given by Archibald Richards of the Tank Corps:

"Inside the tank, the atmosphere was sickening. When you were in action and all the traps are down, the fumes are hardly bearable. There is a thick haze of petrol, gas fumes and cordite... The engine was in the center of the tank and there was a little passage to step around it, but we were very cramped and you had to watch your head. The noise was deafening...we had to make predetermined signals...I had a good stomach, but others were sick... Our officer sat at the front with the driver and signalled what he wanted, and the tank would swing round to face the target. The tank would turn on its own in a wide circle, but with the two gear changers you could turn the tank on its own length. The engine was quite powerful and vibrated the machine somewhat, but it was the movement up and down which was the worst, up and down, this way and that. I had a job sometimes to set on my target, to shoot. I'd just get set on the target and ready to fire and bang, the tank would lurch somewhere, throw me right off."

Though Flers had not proved the tank an instantaneous war winner it was deemed sufficiently significant that an order for 1,000 more machines was made. Next off the production lines came the Marks II and III, again made in the "male" and "female" varieties. These were essentially similar to the Mark I, but lacked the vulnerable steering tail which was not really necessary. The Mark III also featured a marginally improved armor so that in places this was 12mm thick. From this very modest extra two millimeters would begin the long battle between armor and gun which has characterized the story of the tank ever since.

It was the Mark IV tank, first produced in early 1917 and later made in large numbers, which showed the greatest advance to date. In addition to 12mm armor, there was a 70 gallon petrol tank resulting in a 35 mile radius of action. In emergencies an unditching beam on the top could be released to swing down underneath the tracks, so helping the tank to escape from boggy ground. Despite its widespread deployment, and success at Cambrai, the Mark IV still used the clumsy two speed gear box with two secondary gear boxes which required so much effort, and its top speed was still under four mph. A new gearing system and engine had to wait for the Mark V which had a four speed gear box and epicyclic gear system which could now be controlled by one man.

French interest in tanks, or tank-like machines, also predated the war. A scheme for a 75mm gun in a steel box, mounted on tracks, had been put forward by a Captain Levavasseur of the artillery as early as 1903, though this promising suggestion was never built. Experiments with an armored roller and an agricultural-type tractor for

breaching wire were underway in early 1915, but overtaken by the development of true tanks based on Holt-type, tracked, artillery tractors. On December 1, 1915 Colonel Estienne wrote to Joffre suggesting a meeting regarding the employment of "mobile armored constructions for the purpose of assuring the progress of the infantry." Just a few days later it was agreed that the idea should be progressed, perhaps with a tractor to tow a trailer full of infantry as part of the scheme. Though the trailer device was dropped, Estienne went on to work with Schneider to create a true tank capable of about four mph carrying a 75 mm gun and two machine guns. These would first see action in April 1917. Though the Schneider was lighter than its British contemporaries it suffered from two drawbacks which made it a less useful machine. The first of these was the relatively small and low layout of the tracks which limited the performance. The second was an alarming susceptibility to fire. At their first offensive on the

Below: **The end of many tank crew: the horribly mutilated remains of a British soldier beside his Mark IV "Female."**

Chemin des Dames, the Schneiders went forward successfully, but with catastrophic loss. Of 132 machines committed, 76 were immobilized on the battlefield and the majority of these were burned out. As one account observed it was artillery which caused the worst damage:

> "It was hardly dawn yet we drove through Pontavert and on to the road to Guignicourt which, up to the crossing of the Miette, had us run parallel to the front for three kilometers, close to and in sight of the enemy. They found us out approximately halfway through. Numerous batteries opened fire at us... The first tanks had to cross in a column under terrible fire, then proceed along the river for a few hundred yards of chaotic terrain before they could find a place where they could deploy for battle."

As the tanks went on, some were stopped by fire, others went into shell holes, and could only be extracted with extreme difficulty. In some instances, tanks with mechanical problems or damage were in danger of impeding the progress of those following behind. One of the tanks to fall victim to German guns was that of Major Bossut—the wreckage was found by Bossut's own brother:

> "I first saw the almost-charred remains of Sergeant Major Duyff who had been able to crawl about twenty yards away from his tank before dying. Under the tank's very door was my poor brother, largely spared by fire, with a quiet composure on his face; his skull showed a number of wounds. A piece of shrapnel that had entered his chest near the heart and had come out below his shoulder blade

Below: **French St. Chamond tank, seen at Condé sur Aisne, May 1917.**

Above: **French FT17 tanks advance. The two-man tanks were armed with a 37mm gun and were widely used by French and U.S. forces.**

had certainly killed him instantly. There is no doubt that the Major, blown out of the burning tank by the explosion, would have tried to get away from the blaze had he still a breath of life in him."

Interestingly, the Schneider was not the only French tank developed during 1916. A rival project initiated by General Mourret of the army service *Technique Automobile* produced a second design, later to be known as the St. Chamond. It first saw battle action in May 1917. This had thicker armor at 17mm maximum, mounted a 75mm gun and four machine guns, and had a slightly greater speed. Its range was also marginally greater, and it could carry more ammunition. While the St. Chamond thus looked good on paper, its obstacle problems were if anything worse than those of the Schneider. Its nose overhung the track unit and had a tendency to ground—so that its cross-country performance has been aptly described as "woefully inadequate." Nevertheless the 400 St. Chamond tanks built did see considerable action, only a little less in fact than their Schneider cousins.

In retrospect, a more important French tank was the little FT17, or Renault model 1917. This was radically different, being small, light, and with a crew of only two. Most significantly it carried its main armament (either a 37mm or a machine gun) in a small turret on top, capable of a full, 360 degree rotation. The theory was that these light tanks would be employed in "swarms" that would overwhelm the enemy and be difficult to annihilate due to their greater speed and numbers. Though not all were made, several thousand were indeed ordered. The FT17 was also adopted by the US army as its first tank. The Renault light tank first saw action in May 1918, and over 2,000 were in use by the end of the war. A parallel development to the French light tank was the British "Whippet" which also saw use in the last year of war. Though much larger than the Renaults, the British Whippets had three-man crews and were capable of about eight mph. They were also about half the weight of the conventional Mark IV. These proved particularly useful toward the end of hostilities when the more open conditions made full use of their greater speed and radius of action.

Above: "Adalbert," one of the pitifully few German A7V tanks to see action in 1918, traveling by rail flat car.

Perhaps surprisingly German tanks were conspicuous mainly by their absence. The appearance of Allied armor had come as an unpleasant surprise, and only in October 1916 did the "A7V" committee issue a specification for a proposed German tank. This was to have a good cross-country performance, a road speed of about 7mph, weapons to fire in all directions and a trench crossing capability of one and a half meters. This comparatively modest plan for a machine which was little or no improvement on existing Allied types should have been comparatively easy to achieve. Yet the tank manufacture did not receive top priority, and no German tanks were ready for battle until late 1917. More alarmingly the prototype, which was tested from October that year, met with considerable criticism. It was difficult to start, shed its tracks easily, and worse, had a very poor obstacle crossing capability. More work was needed, and the completed A7V was only eventually demonstrated to the Kaiser in February 1918.

As finally completed, the German A7V was effectively a large armored box on tracks. The crew was an amazing 18 men who steered and commanded the machine, manned a 57mm gun, and formed six, two-man machine-gun teams. Though these disappointing Leviathans would see quite a bit of action, total production would not be much more than twenty, at a time when French and British tanks could be counted in four figures. The bizarre consequence was that captured Allied machines would outnumber home-produced tanks in the German order of battle. Unsurprisingly the Germans, therefore, put more effort into the production of the first antitank rifle, armor-piercing bullets, and antitank artillery tactics.

OVER THE TOP

The stereotype of the great battles of trench warfare is that attacks were basically similar, with infantry advancing in lines until cut to ribbons by machine guns and artillery.

To paraphrase Wellington speaking of Waterloo, these assaults came on in the same way and were seen off in the "same old way." Such a description might reasonably be applied to the First Ypres in November 1914 where young German reservists were in the forefront of the attack—and tactics had yet to gain any degree of sophistication. As Private Hamel of the London Scottish reported of a German advance at night:

> "A terrific rattle of rifle and Maxim fire broke out and away in front of us a line of dim figures advanced… We blazed away into them and I

wondered why they lay down in twos and threes to fire back at us. Then suddenly it struck me that they were tumbling over. They made no attempt to rush us, but they still advanced at a steady walk, falling as they came. Flashes spat out along their line. There was no sound—no shouts or cries, only the crackling of rifle shots. The bullets were cutting through the hedge in front of us and slapped into the bank behind us the whole while."

One of the men advancing on the other side of the line at Ypres was the young Adolf Hitler—then an unknown and unsociable soldier with the 16th Bavarian regiment. It was a formative experience, and a noisy one close up:

> "…an iron greeting came whizzing at us over our heads, and with a sharp report sent the little pellets

Below: **A still photograph from the film** *Battle of the Somme.*

flying between our ranks, ripping up the wet ground: but even before the little cloud had passed, from two hundred throats the first hurrah rose to meet the first messenger of death. Then a cracking and a roaring, a singing and a howling began, and with feverish eyes each one of us was drawn forward…"

Yet while it was true that few offensives on the Western Front gained much ground between the winter of 1914 and the spring of 1918, and casualties were often catastrophic, the detail and the tactics, changed remarkably with time. Offensives—even repeated ones over much the same terrain—could be very different. The First Ypres for example, was actually a very different battle to Loos or Verdun, and radically removed from the German offensive of 1918.

As early as the 1920s, the veterans themselves were pointing out that there was far more to trench warfare than common repute would suggest. As Ernst Jünger put it, accurately, if over dramatically:

"One hears it said very often and very mistakenly that the infantry battle has degenerated to an uninteresting butchery. On the contrary, today more than ever it is the individual that counts. Every one knows that has seen them in their own realm, these princes of the trenches, with their hard, set faces, brave to madness, tough and agile to leap forward or back, with keen bloodthirsty nerves, whom no dispatch ever mentions. Trench warfare is the bloodiest, wildest, most brutal form of warfare, yet it too has had its men, men whom the call of the hour has raised up…"

Moreover, the idea that the mental panorama was one of three and a half years of unrelieved gloom does little justice to the resilient spirit of many of those who took part. In retrospect, one muddy battlefield, or dead body, seems much like another—at the time there was genuine conviction that attack was necessary, and frequently belief that enemy collapse or a breakthrough was imminent. Significantly, a number of the most costly battles were not specifically initiated by the commanders

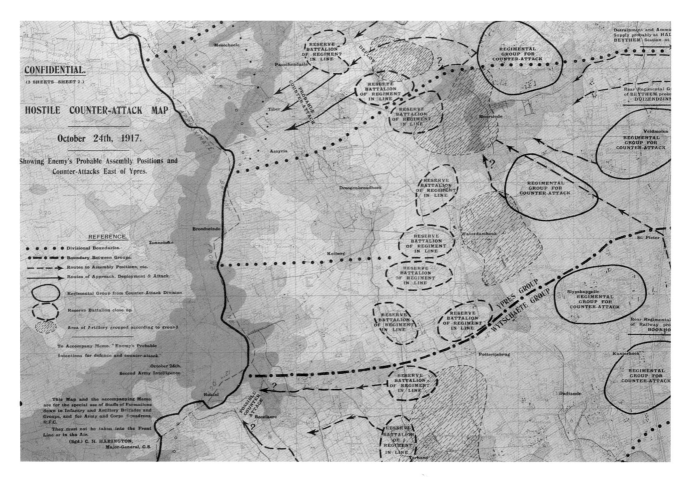

of the armies on the Western Front itself. Some were to support Allies, some to satisfy the demands of opinion at home.

It was also true that the stakes rose insidiously with time and the spending of lives. In 1914, it is arguable that a quick victory by either side might have led to a relatively moderate peace settlement, detrimental no doubt to the citizens of Belgium, Alsace, Serbia, and Russian Poland. But it would have left Europe without revolutionary changes in the short term. As nations dribbled away their life blood, and spent resources yet to be earned, attitudes would harden. The U-Boat war with sinking of ships like the Lusitania, gas warfare, and other atrocities helped to convince the Allied powers that they were fighting for "civilization" against tyranny and oppression. On the other side of the coin, what had been something of an opportunist adventure, ostensibly in support of junior partners, became an issue of national survival. Blockade led to shortages of material, then to literal starvation. The unleashing of social upheaval and Bolshevism in Russia appeared at first like a godsend to the Central Powers, but ended as one more threat to the old order.

Against such a background, it is not surprising that the nature of the trench war changed. Yet the most important motors for change on the battlefield were the minds of the soldiers and scientists, and it has rightly been observed that the interface which conditioned this "modern" war was that between tactics and technology. It is also the case that many of the greatest advances on both sides were the result of trial and error, of imitating enemy methods and copying enemy weapons and munitions. Nevertheless there were good reasons why the trench deadlock could not be broken over the next three years.

Material shortages were a major factor from the latter part of 1914, and through most of 1915. All armies experienced shortages of one sort or another and the "Shell Scandal" was by no means limited to Britain.

The Russians had arguably the worst experience, but even before 1914 was out, the Germans had issued instructions on the husbanding of shells. This was occasioned, so it was said, because "the lessons of war do not agree with the methods and instructions adopted in peace time" and "the maximum output of German factories cannot supply our armies with ammunition to an unlimited amount."

In order to save munitions, German gunners were therefore ordered only to fire at targets that were worthwhile; not to bother firing at night; observe fire carefully; and cooperate fully with the infantry. To make the German position worse the 1914 Austro-Hungarian performance against Russia on the Eastern Front had been at best lackluster. Despite the German victory at Tannenberg, significant resources would be required to prop up her partner. It was, as one

Left: **Hostile Counter Attack map from Ypres, October, 1917.**

Right: **The retreat from Mons, 1914.**

senior German officer put it, like being "fettered to a corpse."

On the Allied side of the line, the gross underestimates which had been made regarding the numbers of guns, shells, and machine guns quickly came home to roost. At one point Sir John French, British commander on the Western Front, was actually convinced that offensive action was impossible. Nevertheless given the desire to relieve the pressure on Russia, and French goading that Britain was not pulling its weight, British offensive action was planned to match French efforts. The result was three deeply flawed British attacks: the hopeful beginning at Neuve Chapelle in March 1915, the "serious disappointment" of the battle of Aubers Ridge, and the fight at Festubert, both in May. At Aubers Ridge, the shortage of munitions was felt from the first. There were only sufficient shells for a forty minute bombardment and it was only possible to fire at maximum intensity for ten minutes. There were enough detonations to tell the enemy that a serious attack was coming, but not enough to cause him severe loss. Attempts to neutralize hostile batteries failed. The Germans manned their parapets in time, and as a result there was no surprise.

The Indian Dehra Dun Brigade was hit with heavy machine gun and rifle fire even as it left its trenches and made no progress. For those who got furthest there was a predictable meeting of vulnerable human force with an immovable object. As a stunned Lieutenant K. Moore of the Middlesex would see:

> "It was a terrible thing to watch line after line crumple up. Meanwhile the trenches were absolutely blocked with the dead, dying, and wounded. If people at home really knew…"

General Rawlinson summed it up surprisingly frankly: "A feeling exists that life is being thrown away on objectives which are not worth it." Whether it was "worth it" depended very much on the big picture.

Writing in 1929, Lieutenant Colonel Kearsey stated that the British could have waited: waited until guns and ammunition were plentiful, waited till training and staff work had improved, and waited until Lord Kitchener's "New Armies" were in the field. Such a course of action could have been in Britain's narrow best interests, but perhaps Russia would have suffered even more seriously than she actually did in 1915.

Neither did material considerations prevent the French from attempting what, with hindsight, might now appear the impossible. At Vimy Ridge in May, Foch's Tenth Army attacked following a four day bombardment, which Sir Henry Wilson would describe as unheard of in the history of warfare—the shells passing overhead in "one steady hiss." It was the beginning of what Foch himself would explain as the application of "destruction" and "repetition." Yet his divisions were repulsed here and elsewhere, as were the British.

During the attack at Loos, gas proved a double-edged sword: both discomforting the enemy and blowing back in the faces of the attackers. As Sergeant Packham of the Royal Sussex related:

> "Just before we had to go over the top, an officer gave me a message to take to the officer in charge of the platoon when they reached the front line. I went up the communication trench which was full of troops which made it difficult to make good time, but I was able to get into our front line. There was a gas officer in the trench. He looked ghastly and all the buttons of his tunic were green as if they were moldy. He was saying that gas was blowing back into our troops' faces. The wind had turned round on us. The German shelling was terrific and the forward troops had gone over the top... The gas was now very thick and everybody was wearing gas masks, just a flannel bag with a mica slot to see through. I had mine on but my mica slot was all steamed up and I couldn't see anything. Also, I was nearly suffocating so I took it off, and to my amazement there were only six of us advancing."

Corporal Moylan of the London Regiment remembered that the actual going "over the top" at Loos was not as bad as expected—a man near him was hit with a machine gun bullet, but in his vicinity the enemy had abandoned the front. Only when uncut wire was encountered did troops get caught. But there were instances when

crowds were decimated. The scene in front of the 15th Reserve Infantry Regiment was catastrophic. As one German observer said, "never had the machine gunners such straightforward work," they "traversed to and fro unceasingly." With the entire field covered in British troops "the effect was devastating and they could be seen falling literally in hundreds."

While the battles of 1915 brought huge casualties and no breakthrough in the west, it would be wrong to assume that no lessons were learned. Both sides were experimenting with new methods of attack. Concentrated bombardment with high explosives offered the prospect of literally blowing the enemy out of the way. Small "bombing" or grenadier parties or shock troops who penetrated a trench system at a single point and then worked along the trenches seemed to offer a less costly alternative to linear attack.

Left: **Fixing scaling ladders in the trenches, the day before the Battle of Arras, April 8, 1917.**

Below: **Germans being rounded up at Vimy.**

Above: **Army Service Corps drivers with their motor ambulance. With open cabs, the goggles were not just for show.**

On the larger canvas several theorists put forward grander ideas which might lead to genuine open warfare. In a French view, translated into English in December 1915 as "A Study of the Attack in the Present Phase of War," Captain Andre Laffarge put forward an influential blueprint for the offensive. According to this synthesis, small-scale attacks were useless as the enemy had plenty of time to prepare new defenses further back. What was needed was a "forward bound" large enough to resolutely swallow the trench system in "a single gulp." The only way to do this was to muster "overwhelming superiority of fire," and to "drown the enemy under successive waves, remembering that infantry units vanish like a handful of straw in the fire." Chances would be much improved by making as many troops as possible "assault troops," and by having jumping-off points as close to the enemy as could be. Best of all the infantry should begin their advance during the artillery preparation.

The essential duty of the first wave was to get as far as possible, preferably at the point of the bayonet, but with the rifle magazine always fully topped up so that the soldiers could take snap shots even on the move. Thorough clearance of all defenses was not to be seen as a function of the first wave: really stubborn points could be isolated and masked, shelled, and dealt with later by a reserve. Second lines of attackers would bring with them machine guns and light artillery for direct support, and would force their way through the weakest points of the defense. Given that "it is impossible for the staff to see clearly what is going on in the struggle," reinforcements had to be preplanned, not directed forward as and when clear information was finally received. By then it would be too late to exploit success. Some of these ideas would lead to dramatic successes: others to the most tragic failures of the war to date.

Though the end of 1915 brought no victory, it was clear that Germany had gained advantages during the last twelve months. Russian forces had been pushed back across Poland, and the many, expensive Allied attacks in the west had ultimately led nowhere. Though Britain was arguably the greatest threat, Falkenhayn now reasoned that it was an attack on France which might pay the biggest dividends. France, he told the Kaiser, "had almost reached breaking point." By causing the French such serious loss that they might wish to end the war, Britain would be left in the lurch and presented with very serious problems in maintaining a foothold in Europe. Russia, already reeling, might well now collapse or sue for peace as well. Quite how such a blow might be struck against France was a more tricky question—the Marne had demonstrated how difficult it could be to work around Paris, and in the north there would be more chance of direct British intervention. Moreover, concentrating sufficient force for ambitious schemes in muddy Flanders would be fraught with difficulties, not least of which was that Germany did not appear to have enough troops.

So the eyes of the German High Command turned elsewhere in the hope of finding places that the French would be so loath to relinquish that in defending them they would cripple their armies irrevocably. The choice seemed to boil down to Belfort or Verdun: Falkenhayn's conclusion being that:

> "Preference must be given to Verdun. The French lines at that point are barely twelve miles distant from the German railway communications. Verdun is therefore the most powerful *point d'appui* for an attempt, with a relatively small expenditure of

effort, to make the whole German front in France and Belgium untenable."

In hindsight the idea that Verdun could have been fought with "relatively small expenditure" seems tragically ridiculous, for the battle that opened in February 1916 and continued until July would set new and unimagined standards for carnage and destruction. Following delays due to bad weather, Crown Prince Wilhelm, commanding the German Fifth Army, witnessed its beginning:

> "Shortly before 8am on February 21, the general commanding the artillery, General Schnabel, and the Corps commanders received their instructions to open fire. In the clear winter air, the thunder of the howitzers opened the chorus, which rapidly swelled to such a din that none of those who heard it had ever experienced hitherto. The enemy, surprised by the annihilating volume of our fire, only shelled a few villages at random. At 5pm, our barrage jumped to his second line, and the skirmishers and shock troops left their trenches. The material effect of our bombardment had been, as we discovered later, rather below our expectations, as the

Left: **Surprisingly cheerful, British "New Army" men by their bell tent. The unusual hair style, short over much of the head with a tuft left in front, was particularly popular in 1916.**

Right: German flame-throwers advancing along a trench on the Marne.

Below: 16th Middlesex on the Somme. Also known as the "Public Schools" Battalion, the 16th Middlesex would have 522 casualties on 1 July. The sandbag "town" behind them was punningly called "White City."

hostile defenses in the wooded country were in many cases too well concealed."

Big bombardments which flailed the ground and killed and wounded many, but failed to dispatch the enemy completely, allowing him to fight back when the infantry attacked, were a theme which would recur many times on different sectors in the next eighteen months. For now there appeared to be only one possible option: to apply more force, and more men.

For a while it genuinely seemed that Falkenhayn's strategy was achieving its ends. French losses were heavy, and certain divisions broke under the strain, leaving vulnerable gaps in the line. On February 25, Fort Douaumont fell— a highly symbolic strongpoint, on a symbolic battlefield. Verdun would also see the application of experimental tactical methods: the use of men of the "Assault Detachment" with infantry guns, flamethrowers, and light trench mortars with the first wave, which in any case was composed primarily of bombers and skirmishers. Attrition, however, worked in both directions and after the first two months of pounding, both sides had sustained more than 100,000 casualties. The continuation of the battle of Verdun into the summer also saw mounting pressure on the British to begin an attack of their own.

THE SOMME, 1916

Perhaps the most familiar image of the Great War is that of going "over the top" on July 1, 1916, the first day of the Battle of the Somme. This cost the British army 57,000 casualties, with more than 19,000 of them killed immediately or later by their wounds. That morning, following huge mine explosions, the men of more than a dozen divisions responded to officer's whistles and clambered out of their trenches to advance across no man's land in the direction of enemy trenches that had already been bombarded for days. They expected little resistance but met shell fire and the rattle of machine guns. Few accounts rival the vividness of that of an officer of the German 180th Regiment, who looked out in the direction of the British 8th Division:

"The intense bombardment was realized by all to be the prelude to an infantry assault sooner or later. The men in the dugouts therefore waited ready, belts full of hand grenades around them, gripping their rifles and listening for the bombardment to lift from the front defense zone on to the rear defenses. It was of vital importance to lose not a second in taking up position in the open to meet the British infantry which would advance immediately behind the artillery barrage.

Looking toward the British trenches through the long trench periscopes held up out of the dugout entrances, there could be seen a mass of steel helmets above the parapet showing that the storm troops were ready for the assault. At 7.30am the hurricane of shells ceased as suddenly as it had begun. Our men at once clambered up the steep shafts leading from the dugouts to daylight and ran singly or in groups to the nearest shell craters. The machine guns were pulled out of the dugouts and hurriedly placed in position, their crews dragging the heavy ammunition boxes up the steps and out to the guns. A rough firing line was thus rapidly established. As soon as the men were in position, a series of extended lines of infantry were seen moving forward from the British trenches. The first line appeared to continue without end to right and left... They came on at a steady easy pace as if expecting to find nothing alive in our front trenches... The front line, preceded by a thin line of skirmishers and bombers, was now half way across no man's land. 'Get ready' was passed along our front from crater to crater, and heads appeared over crater edges as final positions were taken for the best view, and machine guns mounted firmly in place. A few minutes later, when the leading British line was within a hundred yards, the rattle of machine gun and rifle fire broke out along the whole line of shell holes. Some fired kneeling so as to get a better target over the broken ground, while others, in the excitement of the moment, stood up regardless of their own safety, to fire into the crowd of men in front of them. Red rockets sped up into the blue sky as a signal to the artillery, and immediately afterward a mass of shells from the German batteries in the rear tore through the air and burst amongst the advancing lines. Whole sections seemed to fall, and the rear formations,

Above: **The Somme, 1916, New Zealanders in a forward trench near Martinpuich.**

moving in close order, quickly scattered. The advance rapidly crumbled under this hail of shells and bullets. All along the line, men could be seen throwing up their arms and collapsing, never to move again. Badly wounded rolled about in their agony... Within a few minutes the leading troops had advanced within a stone's throw of our front trench, and while some of us continued to fire at point blank range, others threw hand grenades among them. The British bombers answered back, while the infantry rushed forward with fixed bayonets. The noise of battle became indescribable."

Before the day was out, the British 8th Division alone had over 1,900 fatalities. Worst hit in this small area was 2nd Battalion of the Middlesex. This had the dubious distinction of having the greatest distance to go to get to grips with the enemy, a distance of about 750 yards up Mash Valley in the direction of Ovillers. A few of the brave and the lucky made it into the enemy line, penetrated to the second line, then hung for well over an hour before being driven back out. Counting wounded as well as dead, over 600 men of the Middlesex were out of action. According to one eye witness only about 30 men

of the battalion were left in the British front line, fit and well, at the end of the day. When stragglers had managed to extricate themselves from shell holes, and sufferers of minor scratches had regained their place in the battalion, there were still 540 deaths and serious casualties. The commanding officer was wounded but survived. Two months later, in a London hotel, he tried to finish the job himself with a shot to the head, though even then he lingered a week in a coma. Amazingly 2nd Middlesex was not untypical: according to one set of statistics across the whole Somme front 17 battalions had suffered worse that day.

Even in the face of overwhelming tragedy there were men who died with panache. Famously Captain Nevill of the East Surreys died like a sportsman, as his commanding officer's letter to his mother recorded:

"He started his company assault by kicking off a football which his men dribbled right up to the German trench. I have been able to get that ball since, and will of course send it to you if you should want it as a memento of him, but I and all the other officers of the battalion would be very grateful to you if you should allow us to keep it as a regimental trophy, and in memory of your son's gallantry."

It was also the case that the slaughter was not completely one-sided. As the war diary of the 169th Baden regiment shows the battle:

"Early on the 24th of June, the preliminary artillery bombardment began, at first with the light calibers, then progressively going over to medium and heavy calibers, as well as the heaviest mortar shells over the first four lines of trenches. Many dugouts were destroyed. Supplies of food and munitions were possible only through the most determined efforts of the supply troops. Nightly trench raids by English companies during the later nights were repulsed. Early on July 1, patrols of the 4th and 7th companies of the 169th observed and reported the manning of the enemy forward positions. In a state of great expectation, all parts of the regiment were prepared for the enemy onslaught. As soon as the assault lines broke forward they were met by murderous rifle and machine gun fire, such that the attack disintegrated before reaching our lines. Only in trench S2, because of the terrain, were the English successful in forcing a way through. After a sharp counter-attack with hand grenades, however, they were quickly thrown back as well."

The 169th suffered losses of 14 officers and 577 men.

The image of the Somme is a monumentally enduring one: it would be the first time that a full-length movie film was made of a real battle and shown to British audiences. Up until June 1916 official War Office "kinematographers" had made many short films which had helped whet the appetite of British audiences—so much so that 5,000 cinemas were selling twenty million tickets a week. The shock of the film Battle of the Somme was tremendous, and has had a profound effect on the media ever since—for it showed real dead bodies, British dead bodies. It was supposed raise morale, but as cameraman Geoffrey Malins famously claimed it was also "the truth." Some sequences were juxtaposed, one or two even acted for the camera, but as an image of war it was arguably unsurpassed. The comic book heroics that so many civilians had cherished as their picture of the reality of war was very suddenly expunged.

Below: **Stretcher bearers at Pilckhem, August, 1917.**

Above: **Prisoners near Fricourt on the Somme.**

It is not particulary well explained just why July 1 was so catastrophic. For this there seems to be two key reasons: the first and most obvious is that the much-vaunted bombardment simply did not do its job. In sheer numbers, 1,700,000 shells should have been enough, but they were predominantly light projectiles, many of which were shrapnel that burst in the air.

With most of the enemy garrison well below ground, a majority of the Germans survived. Another very important point, less often emphasized, is that once the attack had been launched it was very difficult to alter. Troops were programmed to advance, and so they advanced. Given the communications of 1916, it was almost impossible to change orders or direction. With no way to obtain reliable information quickly, nor to issue new orders in the light of new circumstances, choice was strictly limited. Usually this would boil down to continuing with a pre-planned attack—or abandonment. To quit on the first day of a major offensive which had been months in the preparation was unthinkable—and according to the most recent theory, hesitation to reinforce was the main reason for failed attacks.

One of the best illustrations of this is contained in the dispassionate diary account of Lieutenant V. F. S. Hawkins, serving with 2nd

Battalion, Lancashire Fusiliers. As part of 12th Brigade of 4th Division, the Lancashire Fusiliers were brigaded with battalions of the King's Own, Essex Regiment, and Duke of Wellington's. The advance started tolerably well, and though an enemy barrage was quickly encountered it was "neither deep nor continuous. It moved in concentrated patches, which enabled commanders to lead their sections through with unimportant losses." A more serious problem came when the battalion passed Vallade trench, when oblique fire from the village of Serre tore into the ranks. Even then 2nd Lancashire Fusiliers got away relatively lightly. Then things started to go seriously wrong, mainly because there was no clear information. The commanding officers of both 1st King's Own and 2nd Essex were casualties, as were their adjutants. The Duke of Wellington's and Lancashire Fusiliers "advanced well," and understandably set a cracking pace to get through the enemy barrage and into the attack. Having advanced, runners found it difficult or impossible to maintain contact with the forward units. Orders to halt were issued, but the two battalions never got them and went on "right into the enemy position."

The commanding officer of 2nd Lancashire Fusiliers now attempted to determine the

Above: **Wounded German prisoners being escorted back behind Allied lines.**

progress of the 11th Brigade, so that he could confirm accordingly. Brigadier Prowse could tell him that his brigade had initially made good progress but was now retreating. As to the occupation of Munich trench, he simply did not know. No runner had been able to give precise information, and signals from the front had been confusing. The 2nd Lancashire Fusiliers were now supposed go forward, and with no orders to the contrary, they did so. In the absence of information from other battalions runners were sent out to nearby units. They did not come back.

At 10.47 the wounded Captain Miller of the Duke of Wellington's reached the headquarters of the Fusiliers with the disturbing news that the right company of the Duke's had not stopped, and now disorganized parties of all four regiments were hanging on to part of the German second line. The barrage was now heavy and officer casualties had been particularly severe. Just afterward, a runner arrived with confirmation that the advance had "practically stopped" with severe casualties, and that reinforcements were needed. Official communications with the King's Own and Essex were "entirely cut off," but "confused and incoherent messages" were now coming from wounded streaming back past brigade headquarters that Munich trench had

been reached. At 10.50 a visual signal was received saying that the Essex were held up and that the enemy were "bombing toward them." The Fusiliers sent up fresh supplies of grenades.

The British defenders of the captured ground now withdrew to the base of the feature known as the Quadrilateral Redoubt, or Heiden Kopf, in what used to be the enemy front line. Here the Germans had mounted a skeleton defense and placed charges so that the redoubt could be blown up in case of emergency. This detonation had been activated prematurely, and fragments of various British units commanded by a Seaforth's officer now hung onto it tenaciously, benefiting from covering fire from Lieutenant Brown's company of the Machine Gun Corps. At a considerable cost, this was retained through the afternoon when fire slackened. That night the enemy crept closer, attempting to get machine guns into positions which would sweep the Quadrilateral when daylight returned. In the early hours, the decision was taken that the redoubt, so hard won, was in fact untenable and should be abandoned. The British 4th Division had suffered 4,692 casualties.

This was, and still is, Britain's bloodiest day in the history of warfare. It was also a day on which innocence died. Hitherto, as far as Britain had been concerned, the war had largely been fought by professionals, volunteers, and foreigners. These were people who wanted to go, or had to go, because it was their job. With conscription now in place, the war was going to be fought by pretty well everyone, certainly by most of the young fit male population. About 200,000 British men had been under arms in France and Flanders at the end of 1914. By the end of 1916, the number would be 1.3 million and the two million mark would almost be achieved at the end of 1917. This would be just half of the total strength of the army, for taking into account other theaters and those drilling, convalescing, and guarding at home, the land strength of the United Kingdom would be more than four million. Many more would pass through the army, to their graves, to invalidity, or be discharged for other reasons. Significantly the army now included whole sections of society who had not traditionally been soldiers and many articulate people able to describe the war in literature, poetry, and vivid reports.

Clearly the war was now being fought by the majority rather than the minority. It was also being fought more by Britain. Until mid–1916, France had clearly been the dominant partner on the Western Front. Her leadership in terms of numbers and commitment had been so obvious as to need no formal statement. France planned attacks and called for help, and Britain conformed. After the Somme, and after Verdun, the balance was less obvious. Though Haig had been under pressure to comply earlier, a "Supreme Command" would finally be achieved in 1918. In 1917, French dominance was further undermined by the failure of the Nivelle offensive, the fragility of her army in the face of mutinies, and by the fact that the US, a third major Allied power, would begin to have its own opinions.

The Somme would subsequently be redefined as a "wearing out battle," attrition which would lead to success later. Nevertheless, there is clear evidence that the intention was a decisive breakthrough. This is apparent not only from the outline planning, but from specific details of the battle as it unfolded. For example, large amounts of cavalry was held in immediate reserve, for the express purpose of exploiting gaps punched in the line, or German retreat. Where mounted units were actually pushed forward against an unbeaten enemy, dug in, and fighting back, the results were predictable. As Hugh Boustead with the South Africans would report:

Below: **Collecting steel helmets. The British "shrapnel" helmet, seen here, was designed by John L. Brodie.**

Above: **Deccan Horse, 1916. No longer a "shock" weapon, cavalry still had a job in scouting and pursuit.**

"At daybreak a regiment of Canadian cavalry appeared suddenly out of the morning mist and rain in the valley below our bivouac. With them were two squadrons of Bengal Lancers. Steel helmeted, on shining horses with jingling harness, they presented a superb picture as they rode by with a cheer. A stir of rising excitement swept us; we had visions of a breakthrough into the open plains of Picardy.

The call came that afternoon. The division moved up to Bernafay and Trones Wood in preparation for the attack on Delville Wood. Our brigade crossed the scarred fields through the stricken squadrons. Dead and dying horses split by shellfire, with bursting entrails and torn limbs, lay astride the road that led to battle... Caught by a barrage, these brave men and fine horses had been literally swept from the Longueval Road."

Though Bousted dated this particular incident to July 9, it is rather more likely to have occurred a few days later. The official history records that the Deccan Horse and 7th Dragoon Guards made it to the high ground between Delville Wood and High Wood on July 14, actually managing to capture 32 of the enemy. As their appearance was realized to be premature and counterproductive, they were withdrawn in the early hours of the next morning having suffered 102 casualties to the men and the loss of 130 horses. Nevertheless, the meaning is clear, cavalry was at hand and a breakthrough was the intention. Yet even this apparently suicidal venture bore some evidence of new tactical thinking, as engineers, armored cars, machine guns, and artillery were all intended to be part of an all arms force with the cavalry to achieve the objective.

There were also other brighter spots on the bleak canvas of the Somme. Particularly important progress was marked with the introduction of the tank, but there were other less spectacular tactical improvements. These were the creeping barrage, advances which hugged the tail of the shells, and night attacks. Many of the lessons that the British infantry learned so painfully on the Somme were consolidated in two new manuals, *Instructions for the Training of Divisions for Offensive Action*, of December 1916; and the brief but important *Instructions for the Training of Platoons for Offensive Action*, of February 1917. What was so remarkable about the latter was that it broke finally with the concept of lines of riflemen—more or less spread out—to which specialists might, or might not, be attached. Instead, it promoted the idea of the platoon as a self-contained unit, with each of the four sections expert in a particular field—being respectively bombers, Lewis gunners, rifles, and rifle grenadiers. Now each platoon contained a range of weapons enabling tactical self-sufficiency in a variety of situations, as for example attacking with bomb and bayonet, under cover from the light machine gun and rifle grenades.

Another tactical footnote was the realization that many troops had become so accustomed to trench warfare that they were naturally inclined to throw bombs rather than use their rifles, and were understandably quick to take cover when going forward. The antidote was seen as a renewed emphasis on the rifle and bayonet drill. Unfortunately the enemy also learned many lessons during 1916 and the long battle of the Somme—some of which appeared in a circular by General von Stein as early as October 1916. Ultimately much was learned about the importance of defense in depth, the utility of light machine guns, and positions which were webs of machine gun and sniper posts—difficult to locate and murderous to penetrate.

THE OFFENSIVES OF 1917

Surprisingly the experiences of Verdun and the Somme had left the Allied determination to attack undimmed. Moreover, there were indicators that at last the enemy might be about to crack. The Allies had a superiority of 168 divisions to the 129 German in the West, and in February 1917 the enemy staged a surprise strategic withdrawal on the Hindenburg line. Nivelle, the new French Commander in Chief, who had made his reputation in recapturing much of the Verdun battlefield, was anxious to recommence the offensive. His plan was for a three fold advance; the first phase between the Oise and Avre was rendered obsolete by the German retreat. This left a drive to be executed by the British as Arras with the Canadians on their flank at Vimy, and a French assault on the Aisne at the Chemin des Dames.

The British thrust at Arras that Easter Monday began promisingly enough with a three mile drive into enemy territory under cover of a massive bombardment. Rather more than half of this was

high explosives. The fire would go on for days. German student Willi Bohle was one who rediscovered his religion under the "shell, shrapnel, and machine gun" which sent many of his comrades "streaming to the rear." Only later did Arras bog down into a slogging match. Remarkably, at least one informed witness, Brigadier Lord Loch, suggested that the slow progress after the first push at Arras was because the troops were not accustomed to "semi-open" warfare: "at the commencement we had no men who knew anything about trench warfare and now we have no men who know anything about open warfare." Nivelle, who gambled on the "violence, brutality, and swiftness" of the first blow of his offensive, was dogged by bad weather. His optimistic appreciation was shattered by the reality of a faltering battle and heavy losses to his tanks. With Nivelle's replacement by Pétain on May 15, and French army mutinies, it was inevitable that more of the load would now fall upon the British.

The biggest battle of the latter part of 1917 would be the Third Ypres, commonly known as "Passchendaele," after one of the relatively insignificant villages to be attacked. Nevertheless, Third Ypres was actually far more ambitious, being part of a scheme planned ultimately to clear the Belgian coast and begin a turning of the German flank. One of the preliminaries was General Plumer's assault on Messines by a carefully measured bite, made all the more dramatic by the explosion of huge mines dug by the Tunnelling Companies under the German line. Just getting the explosives into place had been a Herculean and dangerous task of months which the Germans had striven to prevent. As one of the Royal Engineers involved related:

"One day we broke into the top of an enemy gallery, and as the enemy were heard close by, an emergency charge of 15 pounds of gun cotton was tamped and fired near the hole. Actually, while the charge was being lit, the enemy were heard trying to enlarge the hole which they had discovered in their gallery. After the charge had gone up and the mine was reported free from gas, an exploration party was organized and an advance was made into

Above: **British troops in a front line trench near St. Quentin after the German retreat to the Hindenberg Line, April 20, 1917.**

the enemy gallery. This gallery was lit by electric light and when the Germans heard our party advancing they turned on the light. But our officer had foreseen this danger. He had run forward and cut the leads of the lamps well forward of the party, with the result that only the part of the gallery occupied by the enemy was illuminated. Two Germans were seen advancing, one of whom was shot. Both sides then retired, and after two attempts to destroy the gallery with small charges we eventually placed a charge of 200 pounds in position and exploded it, with the result that the German gallery was entirely closed up."

Nineteen mines were detonated on June 7, with an effect that onlookers described as an "earthquake" which quite literally "lifted the ground into the air." Many of the enemy in the front line were blown to pieces or tossed away by the blast. Others were knocked witless running toward the advancing British troops "like jellies" to surrender. Despite resistance, the barrage running ahead of the attackers ensured that the operation was as a limited success, in which the casualties

were lower than most comparable enterprises.

The main offensive, commencing on a 15-mile front on July 31, would be a very different matter. The usual explanations for the huge casualties and minute gains are bad weather and the inability to transport supplies and reinforcements across a battlefield of mud resembling a thick and filthy soup. Tanks often wallowed helplessly and field guns, in General Gough's own words, sank "up to their axles." But it was the quality of the latest German defenses which was the greatest obstacle, and enemy pillboxes were the significant stumbling block. Yet even here there was evidence of the employment of new, if expensive, tactical methods. According to the history of the South Wales Borderers:

"Special attention had been paid during training to the tactical problem of these pill-boxes... one of the machine guns opened fire at close range and was inflicting many casualties, so Sergeant I. Rees led his platoon forward by short rushes till he had worked round to the rear of the position. Then, having got within 20 yards, he rushed the gun, shot one of its team, bayoneted another, and silenced it. Then he bombed the adjacent pillbox so effectively that, after he had killed five of its occupants, the rest, two officers and 30 men, surrendered."

Just how difficult such a textbook assault could be is shown by the fact that Rees was later awarded the Victoria Cross. While casualties to the regiment at Messines had been numbered in the low dozens, the two battalions at Pilckem Ridge lost over 500. It would be a story repeated all along the line. As on the Somme the grinding would go on for months—and, mainly thanks to the new defense system, it would appear that German losses were proportionately lower than they had been the previous summer.

ARMAGEDDON, 1918

By the spring of 1918, attacks were being conducted in a manner totally alien to that at the start of the war. The latest German instructions were contained in a document entitled *The Attack in Position Warfare*. This stressed the cooperation of all arms, but the importance of the individual, every attack "offering an opportunity for independent decision and action even down to the private soldier." Preparations were to be exhaustive, and fresh formations brought up for the actual attack. Artillery was not to pound away blindly for days beforehand—but enemy guns were to be deluged with high explosive and gas on the day of the attack.

The result would be "neutralization" of the enemy artillery without giving away the element of surprise. Barrages against the enemy infantry were to be unpredictable, stopping and starting again with "a sudden burst" thus catching men who had returned to their positions or manned fire steps and shell holes. Guns pushed up in direct support of the German infantry were to be kept under cover until the last moment, then engage machine guns, tanks, or strong points. The infantry attack itself would generally be led by assault detachments, and skirmish lines or further waves of small assault detachments would follow as the situation required. In the air, scouts and bombing machines would match their activities to the ground assault, not giving away the plan by too much activity before the attack. When the attack came, a concerted aerial effort would include ground strafing; bombing of headquarters and rail targets, and driving enemy machines from the sky so as to prevent

enemy intervention in the ground battle. Though less sweeping Allied methods were essentially similar, with an emphasis on small groups of infantry with a range of weapons, accurate surprise "neutralizing" bombardments and better cooperation. Large numbers of tanks gave the Allies a tactical option lacking to the enemy.

What turned the planned German March offensive from a promising idea to a near success were factors external to the immediate battle-field of St Quentin. Russian collapse had allowed a substantial transfer of German forces from east to west, and French shakiness had led to Haig having to take over a much larger sector of the front than hitherto. Hindenburg and Ludendorff were thus briefly able to achieve a local concentration of superior forces. The British command was all too well aware that while much of 1917 had been spent on offensive action, Allied defenses were not yet fully organized on the latest lines. So it was that a "hurricane" bombardment followed by gas and all-out attack led to a significant rupture in once solid lines. Ernst Jünger was in the forefront of the German infantry:

"We crossed a battered tangle of wire without difficulty and at a jump were over the front line. The attacking waves of infantry bobbed up and down in ghostly lines in the rolling smoke... The English jumped out of their trenches and fled by battalions across the open. They stumbled over each other as they fled, and in a few seconds the ground was strewn with dead."

Yet many small knots of defenders did hang on, some of them fighting even when surrounded. While the British lost their gun line and 383 pieces of artillery on March 21, both sides suffered about 40,000 casualties. The British troops going back, alternately fled, marched, and fought, gradually returning to order. As Private Alfred Grosch of the London Regiment called, new positions were dug every time the opportunity arose to slow the enemy advance. Men dug and dug again, often not knowing where they were—and moved off again before the holes were used. Yet after more than three months of stop-start attacks there was growing realization that this new "open warfare" was even more costly than trench fighting. The period from March to June 1918 saw approximately 800,000 German casualties, about as many as had occurred in the

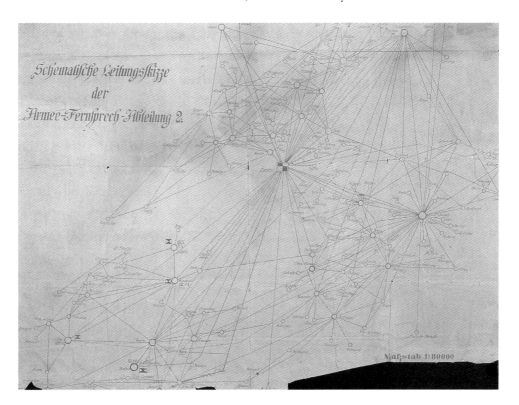

Right: **Map showing German signaling and lines of communication, 1918.**

Left: **Landscape at Pilckhem. The ability to build tracks and light railways through the mud could dictate the pace of advance.**

Right: **American troops soon after disembarkation at Le Havre. The first full U.S. Division to see combat was 1st Division in April 1918.**

preceding nine months. The act of gaining ground, the holy grail of the past four years, now appeared to be losing Germany the war.

By the summer of 1918, genuine "trench warfare" would occur less and less frequently as the Allies went over to the attack. Again there were factors external to the battlefield which played their part—the success of the Allied blockade and the increasing commitment of the US being only the most obvious. Even so it now appeared that both sides had found keys to unlock the stalemate, albeit at horrendous cost.

One of the models adopted by the British would be observations on the Australian success on July 4, circulated to the army as *Operations by the Australian Corps Against Hamel, Bois de Hamel, and Bois de Vaire.* Here it was noted that artillery was not used on "stereotyped lines," but suited to the situation with gas, smoke, and high explosive as needed. Tanks cooperated successfully but above all the infantry "fought its way forward with its own weapons, even when the cooperation of other arms was not available." During the attack, the infantry closed right up to the barrage, reinforcements moving up behind did so in "artillery formation." This translated as spread out, so that shells would cause the minimum of damage. Lewis guns were used directly in support of the advancing sections of the platoons, even being used on the move on occasions.

In August, the first day of the battle of Amiens would be recorded by Ludendorff as the "Black Day of the German Army." Nor was there just one black day, since the horrendous losses of the spring were actually exceeded during the fall. While the British bore the greatest weight during these final attacks, the pressure was over much of the German front—frequently delivered in unpredictable jabs which were difficult to parry, here by the Americans, there by the French. By October, Crown Prince Rupprecht of Bavaria was giving a bleak assessment:

> "Our troops are exhausted and their numbers have dwindled terribly. The numbers of infantry in an active division is seldom as much as 3,000... Quantities of machine guns have been lost and there is a lack of machine gun teams. The artillery has also lost a great number of guns and suffers from a lack of trained gun layers. In certain armies fifty percent of the guns are without horses... The morale of the troops has suffered seriously and their power of resistance diminishes daily."

It was no longer a question of how the war would finish but when it would finish. With the end of the Austrians, and revolution brewing at home, that day finally came on Monday November 11. At eleven in the morning the guns fell silent.

CONCLUSION

The most obvious conclusion about the war in the trenches is that it was not the ossified conflict of the popular imagination. Though the Western Front did not move very far on the map, it did change warfare almost beyond imagination. Previous wars had been virtually two dimensional: armies, lines of men, which could very satisfactorily be depicted on a flat map. By 1918, aircraft had definitively conquered an extra element and a new dimension—fighters and bombers had emerged, which it was now thought might be deciding factors in future wars. The war also moved under the ground, not just in trenches and bunkers, but tunnels and mines. Technology raced ahead on all fronts with the invention of the tank, the beginnings of fast tanks and radio carrying tanks, tracked guns, gas; gas

defense, predicted artillery fire, and planned barrages with new types of shells. There were also many less obvious advances that led to significant changes; the advent of the light machine gun, the sub-machine gun, the anti-tank rifle, and new types of grenade.

The concept of war itself also altered in men's minds. That the war turned normality on its head was indisputable. Frank Richards of the Royal Welsh Fusiliers noted the wry observation that if a man misused his hand grenades to stun fish for the pot, a field punishment was the likely result. The same soldier bayoneting, bombing, or shooting a dozen Germans—his fellow human beings—would be complimented or decorated. Pacifism and conscientious objection had certainly existed before 1914, but they had been very

Below: **U.S. soldiers of the 64th Regiment, 7th Infantry Division, receive news of the end of World War I, November 11, 1918.**

Right: **American troops with the Chauchat light machine gun.**

Below: **Lancashire fusiliers using a pump to drain a front line trench opposite Sessines, near Ploegsteert Wood, January, 1917.**

much minority opinions—often rooted in specific religious beliefs. Between 1918 and 1939 there were signs that pacifism had become a much more general phenomenon. There was also a fairly widespread belief that the trench war had been the war to end all wars, and that future international relations might be regulated by a League of Nations. In retrospect, it is sometimes difficult for us to understand why men had gone to war, and even more amazingly how they stuck at it for so long. Why men fought is indeed asked: but the question is often rhetorical and seldom is an actual answer expected. Captain E. C. Hopkinson, who served with C Company 1st Battalion, The East Lancashire Regiment, anticipated this situation when penning the battalion history in the 1920s. His answer sounds surprisingly modern:

> "Future generations may perhaps wonder what was the mental outlook of the average private soldier as he went to war in August, 1914. Patriotism, in the sense of a demonstrative love of country, might perhaps have seemed non-existent to the casual observer. The curious suppression of this feeling was not of course a trait of the professional soldier alone, but was a national characteristic. It no doubt existed deeper down. The Frenchman set out on his adventures to the martial strains of the *Marseillaise* and shouts of '*La Patrie.*' But who could imagine an English battalion marching to *God Save the King*? Rather did they land in France to *Tipperaray*—a second rate song of the music halls? Perhaps it was that the English soldier took it for granted that his patriotism was beyond suspicion. Whatever it was, he seldom allowed himself to express it, though his acts proved it to be there."

The "mud and blood" school of literature has impressed generations with the sacrifice of those who fought in the trenches. This aspect cannot, and should not, be ignored. Nevertheless it was not "the trenches" themselves that made the war so horrific—indeed, the trenches were designed

Left: **Corporal Harry Aspinall, "Accrington Pal" of 11th (Service) Battalion, The East Lancashire Regiment, pictured October, 1916. Aspinall came through the first day of the Somme and the bloody assault on Serre only to be killed in 1918.**

169

Above: **British wounded, including men of the Grenadier Guards, clad in their "hospital blue" uniforms and red ties. Official statistics would record over two million British and Empire wounded in addition to the dead.**

specifically as a mechanism to save lives on a modern battlefield which was now dominated by more destructive weapons than ever before. Arguably, it was other factors which made the war so costly.

Importantly, the forces on either side of the Western Front would be closely matched for much of the war. In 1914, the massing of the Germans in the west was balanced by a roughly equal number of French, Belgian, and British troops who often had the advantage of fighting from defensive positions. In 1915, French and British attacks with inadequate resources were similarly doomed, with the added factor that in extremis the enemy could transfer men from their much more successful Eastern Front. In 1916, Verdun again demonstrated to the Germans that even with extensive preparation, attacking was likely to be as costly as defending. The Somme, launched specifically to take the pressure from Verdun, brought more British troops to bear and caused significant losses to both sides—but did

not ultimately succeed, as earthworks and defense in depth were not overmatched by sufficiently heavy guns or sophisticated tactics.

In 1917, growing French weakness and the slow build-up of the Americans, failed to give allied preponderance. At the Third Ypres, new attacking tactics were met with new defense tactics on totally unsuitable terrain, in bad weather. With the collapse of Russia in late 1917, early 1918 would offer Germany a brief window of opportunity in which it was again possible to obtain a local and brief superiority. The spring offensive came close to success—but with the greatest irony, open warfare was actually proved to be more costly in casualties than trench fighting had been. Only with the German army depleted, the blockade biting, large numbers of British tanks, and hundreds of thousands of Americans now on the Continent, did the balance tip in the Allied favor. When it did, the latest British attacking methods were shown to be perfectly viable, if expensive in terms of lives.

Above: **German prisoners in England. The uniforms are a mixture of German Field Gray and those provided by their captors.**

Left: **The ruins of Ypres Cathedral in November, 1916.**

171

Another important factor that made the war of the trenches so bloody was that technologies did not advance at the same pace. Battlefield communication advanced more slowly than pretty much any other facet, making fighting the war in "real time" next to impossible. As Guy Chapman so accurately remarked:

> "If the spirit of mechanism had affected the psychology of the fighting soldier, it had also affected that of the staff. Officers of the higher formations no longer went to and fro about the battlefields. When the 2nd Worcestershires made their famous counterattack at Gheluvelt on October 31, 1914, 2nd Divisional Headquarters lay at Hooge Chateau four thousand yards away. When we attacked at Gheluvelt in October 1917, our Divisional HQ lay on the Scherpenberg, as the crow flies near ten miles away, and more by road. Had they been nearer they would not have been more useful: once an attack was mounted, it was impossible to control it. Its fate rested on the skill with which it had been prepared; if the timetable went awry, there was no opportunity for sudden improvisations."

Probably the most reliable form of communication was the field telephone but ironically these were most useful in the static conditions of trench warfare. As soon as a unit succeeded in advancing, it could no longer communicate very speedily, and heavy bombardments would also cut lines. When "electrical communications," as they were called in the idiom of the time, failed, the signallers were thrown back on the quaint methods of former centuries. Foremost among these was the pigeon, as was explained in *Instructions on the Use of Carrier Pigeons in War*, in 1917:

> "Experience has proved that pigeons very quickly become accustomed to shellfire, which does not appear to disturb them at all in their lofts. It thus becomes possible to take pigeons much closer to the firing line. This is usually done by the employment of mobile lofts."

Often the pigeon simply had the message wrapped around a leg or held in a small container, but when secrecy was desired, the pigeon could be induced to swallow it. Yet to get the message back needed special talent as the manual

Below: **Testing telephone lines near the front line at Heninel. The low poles are just high enough to clear the ground, October 23, 1917.**

described: "On arrival at its destination, the bird can be made to regurgitate the tube; but the operations demand a little skill." That the fate of armies could depend on such measures now almost defies the imagination.

Finally, we should not underestimate the extent to which the war was a technological, industrial, and tactical race between nations. We are used to thinking of World War II as such a war—with the strategic bombing, jet aircraft, radar, the atomic bomb, air landing, and special forces, but World War I paved the way in many respects. It saw the harnessing of industry, finance, and labor on a truly monumental scale. A scale indeed which helped to give birth to revolutions. Its important advances were on land, sea, and air, and included chemical warfare. We are shocked to this day but we should not be surprised that such industrious production of killing machines led to such scenes of complete and utter devastation.

Right: **Field Marshal Sir Douglas Haig as he is seldom remembered: seen after the war as patron of the Haig, or "poppy fund," at the British Legion factory.**

Below: **Victory march of the Allied troops, London, July 1919. Royal Navy personnel cross Westminster Bridge.**

INDEX

PICTURE CREDITS

The publisher wishes to thank the following for kindly supplying the photography in this book:

Imperial War Museum (see after each page number for negative numbers) for pages 2 (E(AUS)839), 14 (top) (Q65492), 19, 53 (bottom) (Q57229), 54 (Q675), 58 (Q50721), 62 (Q55394), 63 (Q6460), 65 (Q115177), 73 (Q1332), 79 (top) (Q3990), 79 (bottom) (Q60744), 80 (Q1309), 83 (top) (Q494), 84, 88 (Q2727), 92 (Q50690), 94-95 (Q35849), 111 (left and right) (Q42918A), 114 (top) (E(AUS)4606), 114 (bottom) (Q7823), 118 (Q35290), 119 (Q11586), 123 (Q14945), 124 (bottom) (Q670), 125 (Q69982), 127 (CO1751), 128 (Q33850), 129 (top) (Q8533), 130 (Q69650), 133 (Q65882), 138 (Q7302), 140 (Q6432), 141 (Q2486), 142 (Q6413), 144 (Q69623), 147 (Q70169), 148 (Q60706), 151 (bottom) (CO1155), 154 (bottom) (Q796), 157 (Q5935), 158 (Q3970), 159 (Q4172), 160 (Q8650), 161 (Q824), 164 (Q6049), 166 (Q6850) and 168 (top) (Q57009).

Stephen Bull for pages 21, 24-25, 26, 32, 35, 36, 37 (top), 38-39, 41 (top), 47, 49, 50-51, 52, 53 (top), 55, 56-57 (bottom), 60, 68-69, 70-71, 72, 74-75, 76-77, 78, 85, 86-87, 89, 96-97, 98-99, 100, 103, 105-106, 110, 112-113, 115, 117, 120 (top), 122, 126, 134, 143, 146, 152-153, 169, 170, 171 (top) and 173.

The maps on pages 40 and 61 have been reproduced courtesy of © Richard Natkiel.

The maps on pages 107, 109, 129 (bottom), 149 and 165 have been reproduced by courtesy of the Public Record Office. Crown Copyright material in the Public Record Office is reproduced by permission of the Controller of Her Majesty's Stationery Office.

All other photographs appear courtesy of Chrysalis Images.

For cover photo credits, please see jacket.